EVERYTHING YOU NEED TO KNOW ABOUT

GEOGRAPHY

HOMEWORK

Anne Zeman and Kate Kelly

An Irving Place Press Book

**SCHOLASTIC
REFERENCE**

New York   Toronto   London   Auckland   Sydney

Cover design, Charles Kreloff; Cover illustration, James Steinberg
Interior design, Bennett Gewirtz and Catherine Bontempo, Gewirtz Graphics, Inc.;
Interior illustration, Moffit Cecil

For their assistance in the preparation of this manuscript, we gratefully acknowledge Betty Holmes, Director of UFT's Dial-A-Teacher; Dr. Joseph P. Stoltman; Judy Bock; Dr. Mark Monmonier; Bill Johnson, and Sean McCollum. Dial-A-Teacher is a collaborative program of the United Federation of Teachers and the New York City Board of Education.

Library of Congress Cataloging-in-Publication Data

Zeman, Anne,
Everything you need to know about geography homework/ Anne Zeman and Kate Kelly.
p. cm. — (Scholastic homework reference series)
Includes index.

ISBN 0-590-34172-3

1. Geography—Juvenile literature. I. Kate Kelly. II Title. III. Series.
G133.Z46   1997
910—dc20   96-31171
                                                                    CIP

12 11 10 9 8 7   9/9 0 1/0

Printed in the U.S.A.   09
First Scholastic printing, February 1997

CONTENTS

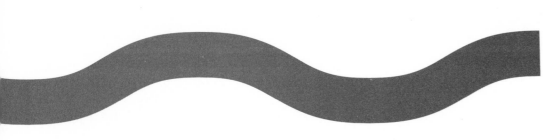

Part 4. Plants and Animals

Part 5. People on Land and Water

Appendix

Index

INTRODUCTION

It's homework time—but you have questions. Just how did your teacher ask you to do the assignment? You need help, but your parents are busy, and you can't reach your classmate on the phone. Where can you go for help?

What Questions Does This Book Answer?

In *Everything You Need to Know About Geography Homework*, you will find a wealth of information, including the answers to ten of the most commonly asked geography homework questions.*

1. Why do particular regions have different climates and what kind of climates are there? The world's climate regions, or biomes, are described on pages 50–56.

2. How do clouds affect climate? The effect of clouds on climate is explained on page 49.

3. Why do we have seasons? Seasons are described on page 14.

4. Where can I find descriptions of U.S. states, including nicknames, state name origins, populations, and capital cities? "The U.S. in Focus," found on pages 120–124, provides this type of information and more.

5. How can latitude and longitude be used to locate major cities and other features on the earth? How to use the geographic grid, which is formed by lines of latitude and longitude, is explained on page 12.

6. What are the different parts on a standard map, including scale, compass, index, legends, and dates? The parts of a standard map are illustrated and defined on pages 27–28.

7. What are the longest rivers in the world? The longest rivers in the world are listed and located on a map on pages 40–41.

8. What are the names of the layers of the earth? A diagram describing the layers of the earth is found on page 30.

9. Where can the border countries of the United States be found? All the countries of the world and the states of the United States are shown in maps illustrated in the Atlas, pages 100–111.

10. What are continents, how many are there, and what are they called? Continents are defined and identified on page 31.

* According to Dial-A-Teacher

What Is the Scholastic Homework Reference Series?

The Scholastic Homework Reference Series is a set of unique reference resources written especially to answer the homework questions of fourth, fifth, and sixth graders. The series provides ready information to answer commonly asked homework questions in a variety of subjects. Here you'll find facts, charts, definitions, and explanations, complete with examples and illustrations that will supplement schoolwork colorfully, clearly—and comprehensively.

A Note to Parents

The information for the Scholastic Homework Reference Series was gathered from current textbooks, national curricula, and the invaluable assistance of the UFT Dial-A-Teacher staff. Dial-A-Teacher, a collaborative program of the United Federation of Teachers and the New York City Board of Education, is a telephone service available to elementary school students in New York City. Telephone lines are open during the school term from 4:00 to 7:00 p.m., Monday to Thursday, at 212-777-3380. Because of Dial-A-Teacher's success in New York City, similar organizations have been established in other communities across the country. Check to see if there's a telephone homework service in your area.

It's important to support your children's efforts to do homework. Welcome their questions and see that they are equipped with a well-lighted desk or table, pencils, paper, and any other books or equipment—such as rulers, calculators, reference or textbooks, and so on—that they may need. You might also set aside a special time each day for doing homework, a time when you're available to answer questions that may arise. But don't do your children's homework for them. Remember, homework should create a bond between school and home. It is meant to enhance on a daily basis the lessons taught at school, and to promote good work and study habits. Although it is gratifying to have your children present flawless homework papers, the flawlessness should be a result of your children's explorations and efforts—not your own.

The Scholastic Homework Reference Series is designed to help your children complete their homework on their own to the best of their abilities. If they're stuck, you can use these books with them to find answers to troubling homework problems. And, remember, when the work is done—praise your children for a job well done.

EVERYTHING YOU NEED TO KNOW ABOUT

GEOGRAPHY

HOMEWORK

THE MEANING OF GEOGRAPHY

Geography Defined

What Is Geography?

Geography is the study of the world, how it works, and how people use and change the world as they live in it. The word *geography* comes from the Greek words *geo*, meaning "earth," and *graph*, meaning "writing."

Geography explores many important questions about where and how we live, including:

1. **What is the earth like?**

2. **Where are things located on the earth?**

3. **Who lives where on the earth?**

4. **Why is one place different from another?**

5. **How do people and places influence one another?**

▶ *A geographer is a person who studies geography. A professional geographer is a person who studies or teaches geography for a living or who uses geography in his or her job. For example, people who make road atlases or people who decide where new toy stores should be built may be geographers.*

The Five Themes of Geography

Geographical thinking centers around five basic ideas, or themes.

1 PLACE
When a geographer says "place," he or she is talking about physical and human characteristics. Physical characteristics are the shape of the landforms and bodies of water, climate, soil, and plant and animal life. Human characteristics include how many people live somewhere and how close together they live, social traits, cultural traditions, and political institutions.

2 LOCATION
When a geographer says "location," he or she is talking about the importance of where one thing is in relation to another. When you study location, you study how physical characteristics (such as harbors, rivers, fertile plains, and mountainous terrain) affect human settlement and the way places are used.

3 HUMAN AND ENVIRONMENTAL INTERACTION
When a geographer talks about human and environmental interaction, he or she is talking about the changes people have made in their environment and the changes they continue to make.

4 HUMAN MOVEMENT
A geographer who studies human movement follows the routes people take when they move from one place to another and tries to explain why these movements are necessary. He or she also studies the effect of human movement on the areas where people move and settle.

5 REGIONS
A geographer thinking about regions looks at what makes one area different from another. To do that, he or she studies physical and human characteristics to see where they change.

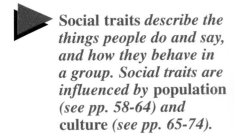 *Social traits describe the things people do and say, and how they behave in a group. Social traits are influenced by population (see pp. 58-64) and culture (see pp. 65-74).*

Geography and You

You don't need textbooks or classroom teaching to begin learning and using geography. In fact, you use geography every day—probably without realizing it.

Mental Maps and Sketches

Mental maps are maps you picture in your mind.

Close your eyes and imagine the inside of your bedroom. Where is the bed? How do you get from the bed to the bedroom door? Once you're at the door, which way do you go to get to the kitchen? How about from the kitchen to the front door? From your home to your school, playground, park, or grocery store?

If you are able to picture places in relation to one another, you are creating mental maps. Mental maps can be of any place, large or small. You will use mental maps all your life to help you understand where you are compared to other parts of your world.

A rough drawing of a mental map is a *map sketch*. If you draw your mental map on paper or on your computer, for example, you will have made a map sketch.

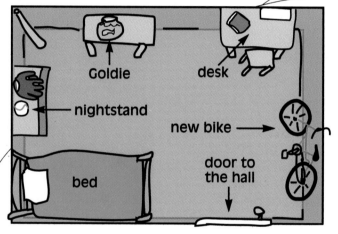

Our first mental maps are usually of our homes.

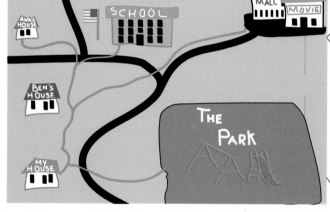

As we grow older, we create new maps to include neighborhoods and parks.

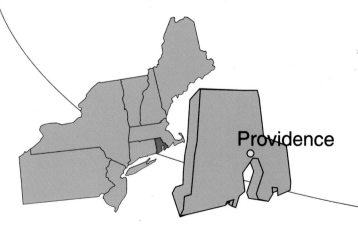

With more knowledge of the world, we are able to locate ourselves in larger areas. For example, we can think of our town within our state, our state within our country, our country within the world.

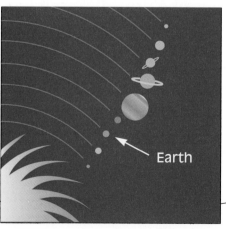

With still more knowledge, we can picture the earth in the solar system, the solar system in the galaxy, and the galaxy in the universe.

4

The Geography of Geography

Geography is about the "where" of things, so it's an important part of many subjects, including biology, weather sciences, history, and geology. Today, geographers usually study the geography important to one branch of learning. Among the many subfields of geography are:

1. **Agricultural geography, the study of farming in different parts of the world.**

2. **Biogeography, the study of plants and animals in different geographic locations and climates.**

3. **Cartography, the science of making maps.**

4. **Climatology, the study of world climates.**

5. **Cultural geography, the study of people and their ways of life in different parts of the world.**

6. **Geomorphology, the study and measurement of landforms on the earth's surface and under water.**

7. **Historical geography, the study of how geography affected historical events.**

8. **Industrial and marketing geography, the study of locations for businesses and factories and how particular locations can benefit or hurt them.**

9. **Meteorology, the study of daily weather, including air temperature, precipitation (rainfall, snowfall, etc.), and winds.**

10. **Political geography, the study of nations and states, including their natural habitats, cities and farms, and populations.**

11. **Resource geography, the study of the location of natural resources and the conservation of those resources to meet human needs.**

12. **Urban geography, the study of how cities develop and how they work.**

GALACTIC ADDRESS

U. R. Here
555 Nutley Avenue
Mapton, Massachusetts

U.S.A.

North America

Northern and Western Hemispheres

Earth

Solar System

Milky Way Galaxy

Universe

A good first step toward making a mental map of yourself within the universe is to write your galactic address.

Geographical Thinking

Picture yourself in Antarctica. What do you see? What are you wearing?

Now picture yourself near the equator. Now what do you see? Are you wearing a parka and snow pants?

You probably already know many geographical words and phrases that produce clear mental pictures. When you think "cold," for example, do you think "north," "south," "east," or "west?" If you live in North America, which direction makes you think "hot?" What do you picture when you think "mountain," "valley," "city," or "swamp?"

Geographical thinking is the ability to think about places and their characteristics. If Antarctica makes you think of a cold place or the equator of a hot one, you are thinking geographically.

Geographical thinking helps you select the appropriate clothes for climate and weather conditions, among other things.

The First Geographers

The first geographers were people who, like you, made mental maps and thought about things geographically. However, they didn't stop there. They traveled around, remembered what they saw, and reported their experiences so other people could learn from them.

Early humans who followed animal migrations in order to hunt food might be considered the first geographers. So, too, might those people who left their homelands to explore unknown areas and, later, returned to tell of their discoveries.

 ## The First True Geographer?

Thales (c. 640 B.C.–550 B.C.) was a man who lived on the shores of the Aegean Sea in Greece more than 2,500 years ago. He established methods for observing places. Thales traveled widely. He journeyed to markets far from his home to trade goods. Along the way, he wrote down all the new things he saw and learned. He also described a way to measure the distances and directions that set one place apart from another. His method was much like the systems of miles and kilometers we use to measure distances today. His information helped later geographers make accurate globes and maps (see p. 12). Because Thales was so careful about his observations, many scholars consider him one of the first true geographers.

 The ancient Greeks were the first people to make a specific list of things to observe about places, such as the distance from other places or landmarks, the number of people at the place, the number of buildings, the source of water, etc. Because of their attention to detail and careful descriptions, they are considered the first real geographers. The Greeks were also the first people to develop the theory that the earth is round, a theory proved to be true hundreds of years later.

REPRESENTING THE EARTH: GLOBES, PROJECTIONS, AND MAPS

 1 Globes

Looking at Earth

A map of the solar system shows the earth in relation to the sun and the other planets.

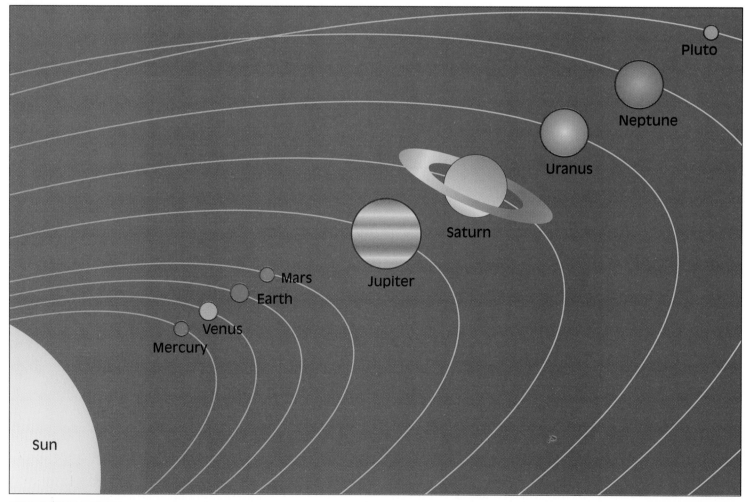

The solar system

Like the other planets, the earth is shaped like a sphere. From outer space, it looks like a disk covered by clouds.

Photograph of the earth from outer space shows water and land formations, as well as cloud cover.

But a photograph can show only half the earth—or one **hemisphere** (see p. 10). To show the whole earth, we use a **globe**, or a sphere-shaped model of the earth. Although it doesn't show all the cloud formations and wind patterns in the atmosphere, it does show the land and water formations on the earth's surface. Globes also help us understand natural events, among them day and night and the seasons.

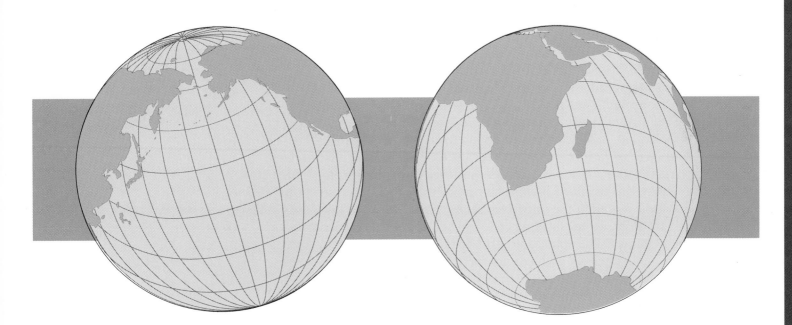

Globes show the water and land formations on the earth's surface.

Inventing the Globe

You can tell by photographs taken from space that the earth is round. But, if you look out a window at school or home, the surface of the earth appears mainly flat.

Yet more than 2,000 years before photography from space was possible, the ancient Greek geographers relied on observation and mathematics to figure out the shape and size of the earth. They made the first globes to show what the earth is like.

Lines of Longitude and Latitude

The ancient Greeks also used their globes to think about the location of places on the earth. They divided the globe into 360 segments, called *degrees*. They used vertical lines called *longitude* to mark off the 360 parts. Lines of longitude, also called *meridians*, are still used today to locate places on the earth, and to measure the distances between places. They can be seen on most globes.

The *prime meridian*, or 0 degrees (0°) longitude, was agreed upon in 1884. It passes through the site of the Royal Naval Observatory in Greenwich, England. Distance is measured east and west of this line. Longitude lines east of the prime meridian are numbered 1° through 179°. This is the *eastern hemisphere.* Longitude lines west of the prime meridian are also numbered 1° through 179°. This is the *western hemisphere.* The 180° line, reached by traveling east or west from the prime meridian, is exactly halfway around the earth from the prime meridian. Much of this line of longitude is used also as the *international date line* (see p. 15).

The ancient Greeks also drew lines to divide the earth horizontally. These lines are called *lines of latitude* or *parallels.* Latitude is measured from the *equator*, or 0 degrees (0°) latitude. Latitude lines are numbered from 0° to 90° from the equator to the north pole. The part of the earth from the equator to the north pole is called the *northern hemisphere.* Latitude lines are also numbered 0° to 90° from the equator to the south pole. The part of the earth from the equator to the south pole is called the *southern hemisphere.*

The northern hemisphere is divided into the tropics and temperate zone at the Tropic of Cancer, a line of latitude that runs parallel to the equator at 23°30′ north latitude. The temperate zone runs from 23°30′ to the Arctic Circle, a line of latitude located at 66°30′ north latitude. In the southern hemisphere, the Tropic of Capricorn, located at 23°30′ south latitude, divides the tropics from the southern temperate zone. The temperate zone ends at the Antarctic Circle, or 66°30′ south latitude.

Lines of *latitude* run parallel to each other; that means they never meet.

Arctic Circle

Antarctic Circle

lines of longitude

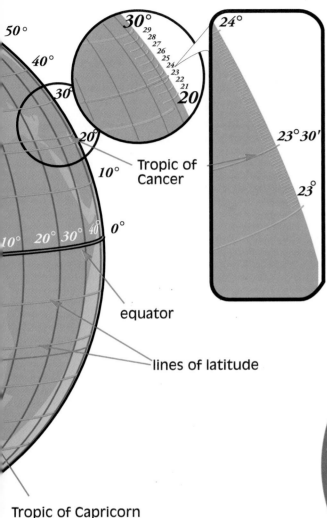

prime meridian

50°

40°

30°

20°

10°

10° 20° 30° 40° 0°

30°
29
28
27
26
25
24
23
22
21
20

24°

23°30'

23°

Tropic of Cancer

equator

lines of latitude

Tropic of Capricorn

Degrees of longitude and latitude are divided into measures called minutes, and marked by the symbol ´. Like minutes in an hour, there are 60 minutes (60´) in a degree of longitude or latitude. Minutes are divided into seconds, and marked by the symbol ´´. There are 60 seconds in each minute of latitude or longitude.

The Two North Poles

The spot where the lines of longitude meet at the northernmost point of the globe is called the north pole. It is also called **true north**, or **geographic north**.

There is another north pole, called **magnetic north**. The magnetic north pole is not located in quite the same place as the geographical north pole, although they are very close. The difference between the location of the true north and magnetic north poles is shown on most globes.

You can find the magnetic north pole with a compass. A compass is made of a magnetized needle held up so that it turns freely. Because the earth itself is a huge magnet, no matter what direction you're going, the compass needle always points to magnetic north.

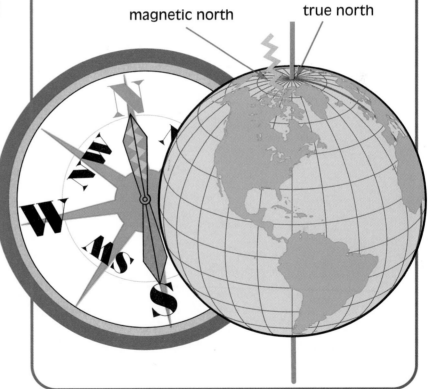

magnetic north   true north

REPRESENTING THE EARTH: GLOBES, PROJECTIONS, AND MAPS

11

GEOGRAPHERS IN ANCIENT GREECE

Greek geographers established the science of making highly accurate globes. The globes are based on some of the most important discoveries made by early Greek geographers.

Eratosthenes of Cyrene (c. 280–200 B.C.) used math and his knowledge of round objects (spheres), to measure the circumference of the earth. His measurement was close to the measurement used by scientists today (24,902 miles; 40,075 kilometers).

Hipparchus (born c. 150 B.C.) refined measurements for ***latitude*** and developed measures for ***longitude*** (see p. 10). He was the first to divide the equator into 360 degrees. Hipparchus also divided the world as he knew it into climatic zones (see p. 50) and drew the first known map of the night sky.

Strabo (60 B.C.-A.D. 25) described his travels through Europe, North Africa, and western Asia in a work called ***Geographia***. Written as 17 books, ***Geographia*** describes in detail the world as the Greeks of his time knew it.

Claudius Ptolemy (2nd century A.D.) wrote an eight-volume book, also called ***Geographia***. In it, he described in terms of longitude and latitude (see p. 10) all the places in the world that were known to the Greeks of this time.

The Geographic Grid

Lines of latitude and longitude form a ***geographic grid***.

The geographic grid makes it possible to identify points on the earth and record their exact locations north or south of the equator and east or west of the prime meridian.

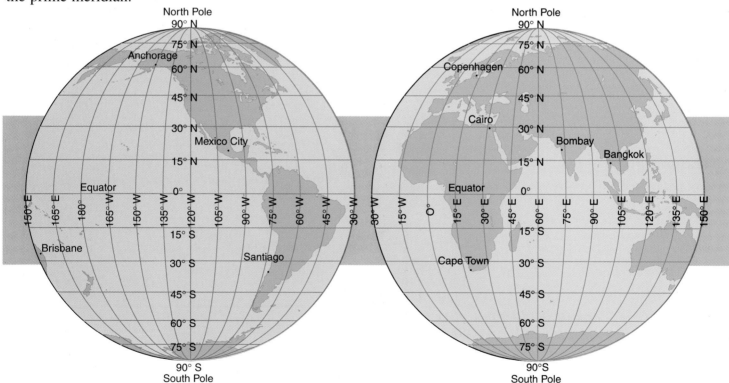

Using coordinates, or points of latitude and longitude, you can locate the places on the earth's surface, including Anchorage, Alaska (61° north latitude, 150° west longitude), Bangkok, Thailand (14° north latitude, 100° east longitude), Bombay, India (19° north latitude, 73° east longitude), Brisbane, Australia (27° south latitude, 153° east longitude), Cairo, Egypt (30° north latitude, 31° east longitude), Capetown, South Africa (34° south latitude, 18° east longitude), Copenhagen, Denmark, (56° north latitude, 12° east longitude), Mexico City, Mexico (19° north latitude, 99° west longitude), and Santiago, Chile (33° south latitude, 71° west longitude).

Light on Earth

Light on earth is a result of our planet's position in relation to the sun and moon. Our position in space results in such events as day and night, the seasons, solstices, eclipses, and tides.

Day and Night

A globe and a lightbulb illustrate how day changes into night. Only half the surface of the globe is covered in light at any time.

As the globe rotates on its axis, the part of the surface that is lighted changes.

Just like the globe in the example, the earth rotates on an axis. As a particular place on the earth rotates out of the sunlight, night falls. As that place rotates back into the light, day dawns.

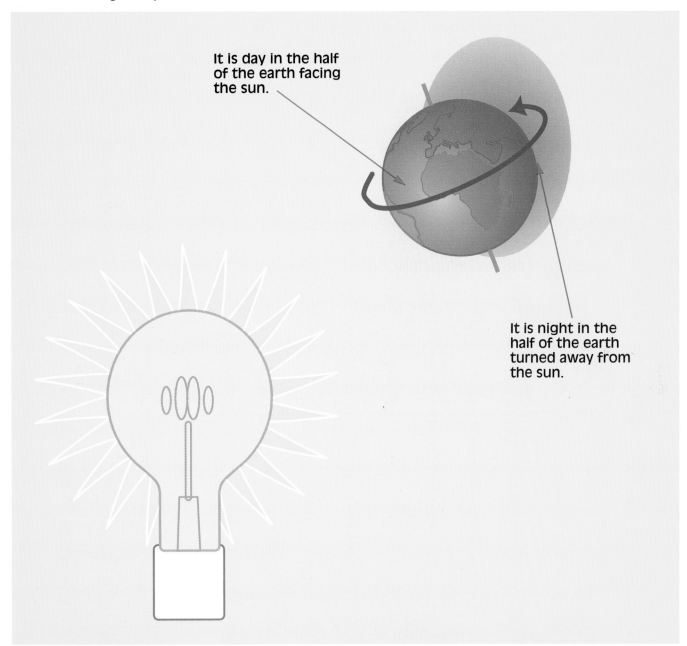

It is day in the half of the earth facing the sun.

It is night in the half of the earth turned away from the sun.

A lightbulb shining on a globe shows how the earth is lit by the sun. Half of the surface is covered by light, the other half is in shadow. As the earth rotates on its axis, every point on the earth moves from the light, or day, to shadow, night, and back again.

The Seasons

A globe and a lightbulb can also illustrate how the seasons change. Earth not only rotates on its axis, it also orbits the sun. The angle of the axis is tilted in relation to its orbit. When the earth is positioned so that the northern hemisphere is tipped toward the sun, it is summer there and winter in the southern hemisphere.

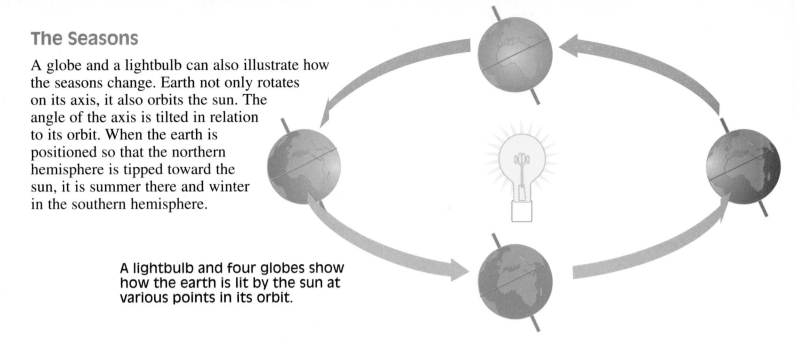

A lightbulb and four globes show how the earth is lit by the sun at various points in its orbit.

Eclipses

Occasionally the light from the sun or the sunlight reflected off the moon is kept from hitting the earth, or *eclipsed*, by the position of the earth and moon in relation to the sun.

A *solar eclipse* occurs when the moon passes between the earth and the sun. People standing in the shadow see the moon pass in front of the sun, blotting out its light.

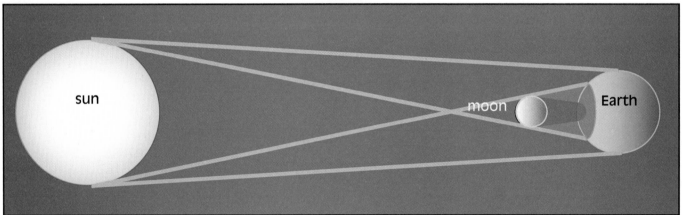

solar eclipse

A *lunar eclipse* occurs when the earth passes between the sun and the moon. People on the side of the earth facing the moon see the moon pass from sunlight into the shadow cast by the earth.

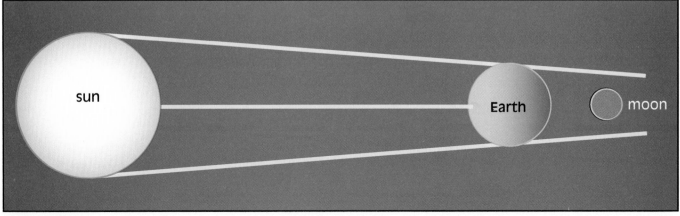

lunar eclipse

The 24 Hour Globe:
Time Zones

In addition to lines of longitude and latitude, the globe is marked off into 24 *time zones*. The time zones run in the same direction as the lines of longitude, and begin at 0 degrees (0˚), or the *prime meridian*. The time zone that lines up roughly along 180˚ longitude follows the *international date line*. Places to the east of this line are a calendar day behind places to the west. If you fly from west to east over the international date line on Saturday, you fly into Friday. You gain one day on your trip.

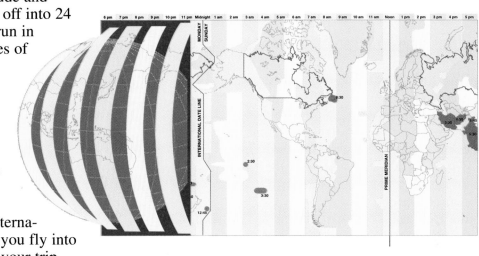

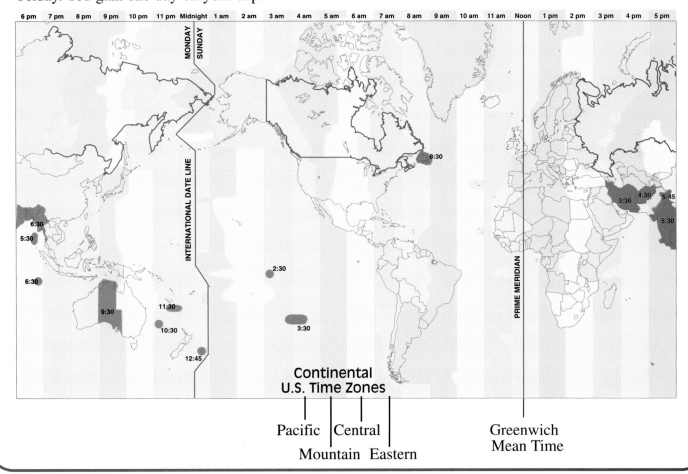

Continental
U.S. Time Zones

Pacific Central
Mountain Eastern

Greenwich
Mean Time

2 Maps

What Is a Map?

A *map* is a picture of a place on a flat surface. Most maps show a place drawn from above.

Different types of maps show different types of information, such as natural features, where humans live, historical and modern political boundaries, centers of industry, and variations in climate and weather.

Map Projections

Imagine peeling the surface off a globe and laying it down flat. It would form a map with a very unusual shape.

Globes accurately show sizes, locations, and distances on the earth because the earth, like a globe, is roughly a sphere. Because they are flat, maps do not show the round earth exactly as it is shown on a globe.

In order to make maps, mapmakers use *projections* based on the geographical grid (see p. 12). In order to take the grid from a globe and open it flat on a map, the grid must be changed somewhat. These changes affect the accuracy of maps.

Standard map projections are created to represent the geographic grid as accurately as possible on flat surfaces. In inventing projections, mapmakers have four major concerns: area, direction, distance, and shape.

When mapmakers make projections, they must decide which elements need to be most accurate on their maps. If a map is going to be used to measure the distance between places, a mapmaker will choose a projection that shows the size of land and water areas as accurately as possible to scale. If a mapmaker needs to show direction and the shape of the land and water areas, he or she will choose a projection that depicts those features most accurately.

Mapmakers' Concerns

area	**The size of land and water areas in relationship to each other.**
direction	**North, south, east, and west compared with their true location on the geographic grid.**
distance	**The distance on a map relative to the earth's surface, called scale.**
shape	**The shape of land and water areas compared with their shape on the earth or a globe.**

Some Common Map Projections

Conic
: Used for mapping a large piece of the earth's surface, it shows accurate distance, direction, and shape for the limited area mapped.

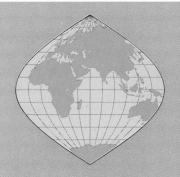

Interrupted
: Shows accurate area and shape. Oceans have (equal area) open, pie-shaped interruptions to adjust for distance.

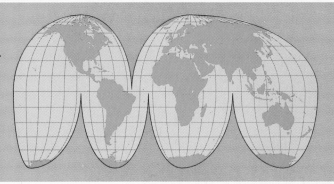

Mercator (cylindrical)
: Shows accurate direction, but land and water areas are greatly distorted toward the north and south poles.

Polar (azimuthal)
: Used for mapping hemispheres instead of the whole earth; shows accurate distance and direction, but shape and size become more and more distorted toward the edges.

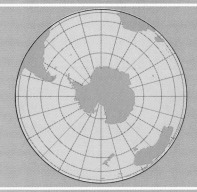

Robinson (oval)
: Shows accurately the shape and size of continents, but the water areas are expanded to fill the extra space.

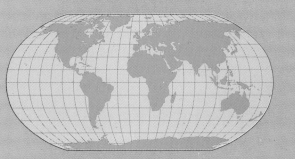

How Projections Are Made

Put a projector light inside a globe. The spaces formed by the geographic grid when **projected** from the globe onto a flat screen will change as the projector light is moved. While the location of a city is likely to fall in the same place on the globe and its projection, the sizes and shapes of countries and continents will change as the distances away from the center of the projected image change. Areas on the edges of the map appear stretched as they are flattened in the projection.

When cartographers make maps, they use mathematical calculations to project the geographic grid (see p. 12) onto paper.

Natural Features

Natural features are features on the earth's surface that were not made by humans. These features include nonliving things (rocks, minerals, soil, water, and atmosphere) as well as living things (plants and animals).

Physical Features

Earth's nonliving, or **physical**, features include mountains, plains, rivers, lakes, and oceans. The earth's physical features are constantly changing. A number of forces, such as erosion and weathering, gradually wear down the earth's surface. Other forces, such as fire, earthquakes, and volcanoes, make almost instant changes (see pp. 32-33).

Atmospheric Features

The earth's nonliving features also include **atmospheric** conditions, or climate and weather. Climate is the usual weather in a place over a long time period. It, along with physical features, determines which plants and animals can live in a particular place (see pp. 43-49).

Living Features

Earth's living features are its plants and animals, including humans. Different plants and animals thrive in different natural regions, or **biomes** (see pp. 50-56). Biomes are large environments that share the same general temperature and annual rainfall.

Human-made Features

Human-made features are features on the earth's surface created by human beings—for example, buildings, monuments, parks, roads, fields, and landfills.

 Cartography *is the art of making maps or charts. People who draw maps are called* cartographers. *The words come from the Latin* carta, *meaning "map," and the Greek* graph, *meaning "writing."*

The First Maps

No one knows for certain who made the first maps or what those maps looked like. But we know that humans have been making maps for thousands of years. Scratched into sand, painted on animal skins, carved into wood, or drawn on rock walls, maps helped people avoid danger, find good hunting grounds, and locate clean water. The ancient Egyptians even supplied maps to tax collectors to help them along their routes.

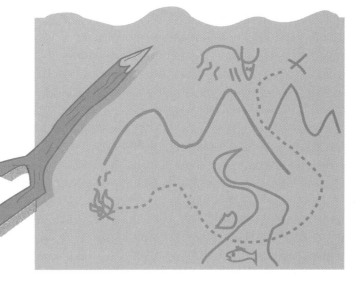

More than 2,000 years ago, Europeans were drawing maps to help them navigate at sea. Called *charts*, these maps of waterways were drawn on skins and stones, carved in wood, or engraved into clay—in much the same way as land maps were made.

Polynesian islanders in the Pacific Ocean made charts out of palm leaves woven through reeds. The pattern of the weaving showed ocean currents and wave directions. Shells were attached to the reed charts to show where islands were located.

The oldest maps that exist today were made in the ancient Middle Eastern civilization of Babylon. These maps are more than 4,000 years old, and are etched into large clay tablets.

Three Basic Kinds of Maps

Political Maps

Political maps show how humans have divided up the earth's surface. They show borders between countries, the locations of cities and towns, building sites, neighborhoods, settlement plans, roadways, and other human-made features.

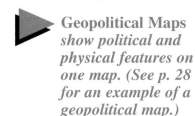 **Geopolitical Maps** *show political and physical features on one map. (See p. 28 for an example of a geopolitical map.)*

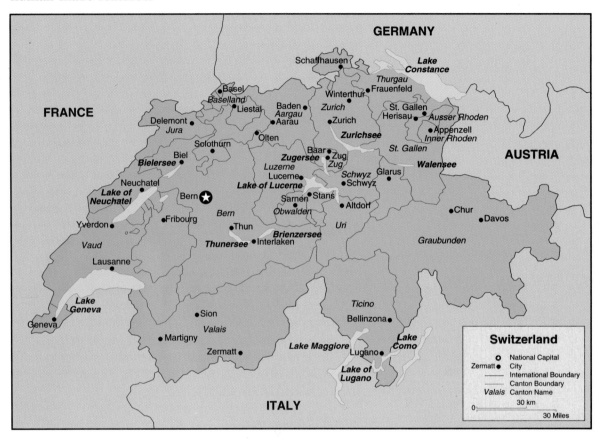

This political map of Switzerland shows the countries it borders, as well as its cantons (states) and major cities.

Physical Maps

Physical maps show the land formations and water on Earth's surface. Physical maps show mountains, valleys, plains, oceans, rivers, and lakes. They can also show locations of natural plant life, water currents, and wind patterns.

This physical map of Switzerland shows variations in the elevation of the land, as well as the location of major rivers.

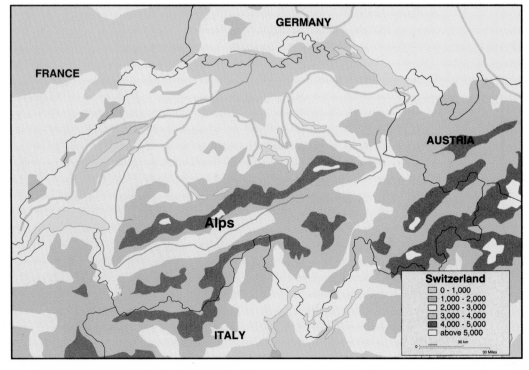

Cultural Maps

Cultural maps show patterns of ethnic groups, religious practices, languages spoken, customs, educational levels, and recreational choices.

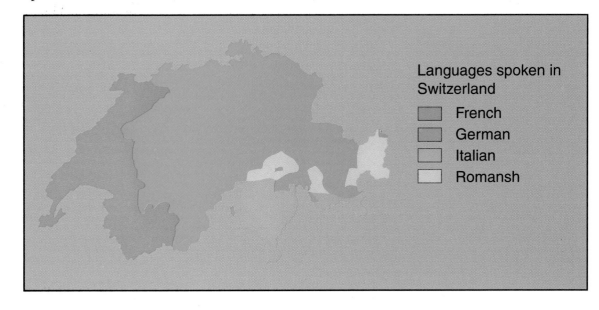

Languages spoken in Switzerland

☐ French
☐ German
☐ Italian
☐ Romansh

This cultural map of Switzerland shows where different languages are spoken within the country.

Charts

Charts are maps of bodies of water. Sailors use them to navigate in open ocean waters as well as on lakes and in shallow bays, inlets, and rivers. Charts show water depths, currents, and physical features found below the surface of the water. They also locate ports and places to anchor safely, as well as buoys, lighthouses, and other aids to seafarers.

The depth of water is shown in feet on this sample chart.

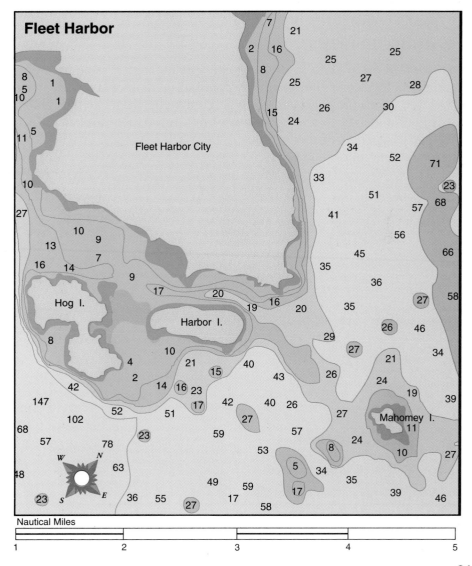

Fleet Harbor

Fleet Harbor City

Hog I.

Harbor I.

Mahomey I.

Nautical Miles

Maps for Special Uses

Relative Location Maps

Relative location maps show the position of a place in relation to its surroundings. For example, such a map might show where a specific place is located in relation to the rest of the world.

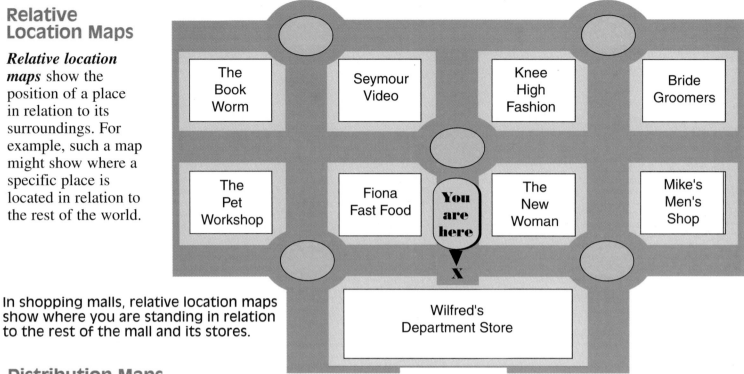

In shopping malls, relative location maps show where you are standing in relation to the rest of the mall and its stores.

Distribution Maps

Distribution maps show how things are spread out across an area or throughout the world. For example, distribution maps may show where sheep are raised on all the continents or where oil wells are located in Oklahoma. Distribution maps can also show where rain forests and timber mills are located, what kinds of rocks make up the earth's surface, or where bookstores are located in your home town.

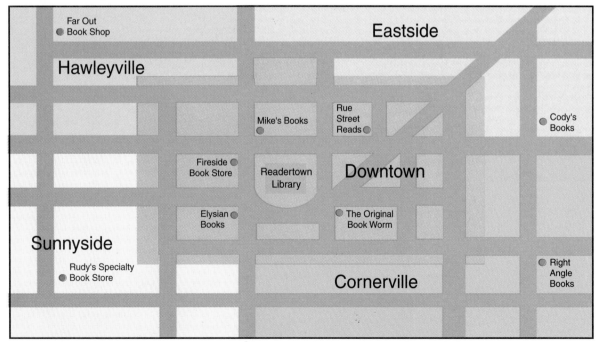

This distribution map shows the location of bookstores in Readertown, USA. According to the map, most bookstores are downtown, and the rest of Readertown's bookstores are evenly distributed in the residential neighborhoods.

Topographic Maps

Topographic maps show physical features, and are often drawn showing *contours*, or lines that show differences in elevations. Any topographic map drawn to show contours may also be called a contour map.

This section of a topographic map shows color-keyed contours, as well as a variety of physical features: rivers, roads, railroad tracks, bridges, and an air strip.

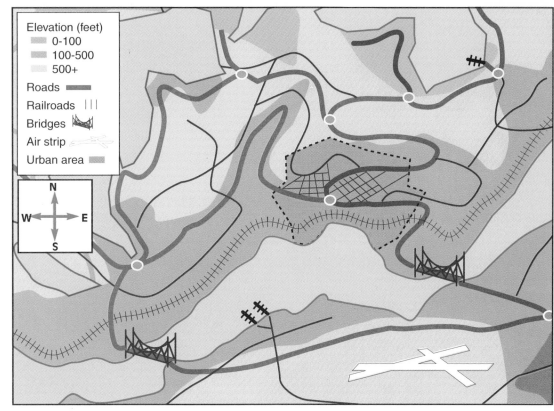

Elevation (feet)
0-100
100-500
500+
Roads
Railroads
Bridges
Air strip
Urban area

N
W   E
S

Climate and Weather Maps

Climate and weather maps show how and where climatic and weather conditions occur across a region or throughout the world.

Weather map illustrating a fall day in the United States

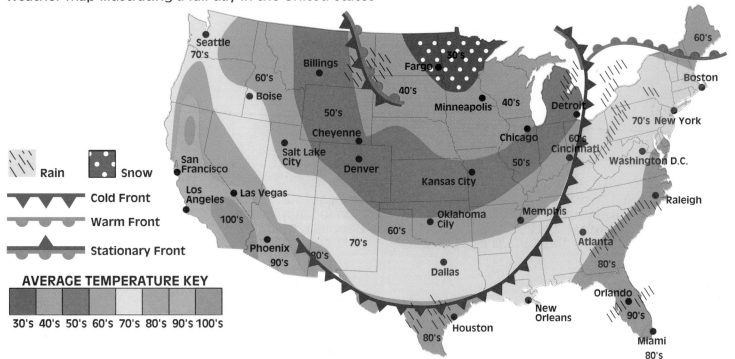

Rain   Snow
Cold Front
Warm Front
Stationary Front

AVERAGE TEMPERATURE KEY
30's 40's 50's 60's 70's 80's 90's 100's

Seattle 70's
Billings
Fargo
60's
Boise
Minneapolis
50's
40's
40's
Detroit
60's
Boston
Cheyenne
Chicago
70's New York
Salt Lake City
Denver
50's
Cincinnati
Washington D.C.
San Francisco
Kansas City
60's
Los Angeles
Las Vegas
Memphis
Raleigh
100's
Oklahoma City
Atlanta
Phoenix
90's
70's
Dallas
80's
New Orleans
Orlando
90's
Houston
80's
Miami
80's
60's

Time Zone Maps

Time zone maps show how the earth is divided into different time zones. (See p. 15 for an example of a time zone map.)

ALTERED STATES:
Cartograms

Cartograms are diagrams in map form. The places on a cartogram are drawn in mathematical proportion to show how much of a particular thing is found in each area mapped.

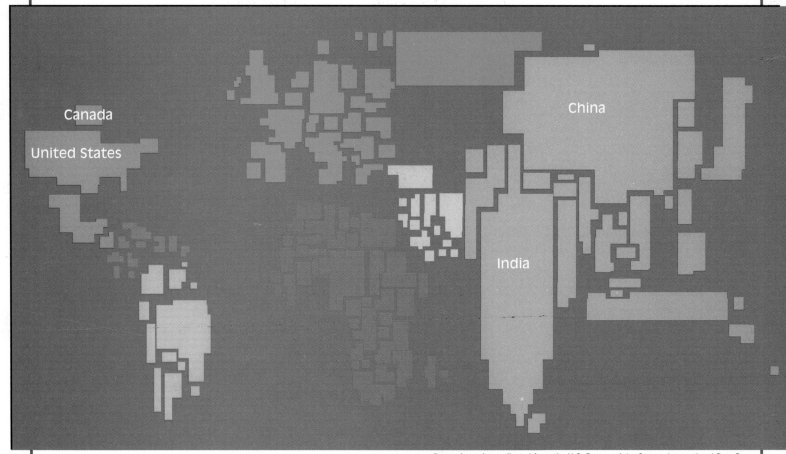

Drawn from data collected from the U.S. Bureau of the Census International Data Base

A cartogram of world population shows China and India as much larger than North American and European countries. Anyone looking at this cartogram can tell at a glance that there are more people in China than in the United States and Canada combined.

Written References:

Geographical Dictionaries and Almanacs

Maps and globes are the most important tools you will need to do your geography homework, but *geographical dictionaries* and *almanacs* are very useful, too.

Hoth·am, Mount \-'häth-əm\. Mountain in the Darg Plateau, E Victoria, SE Australia, SW of Mt. Kosciusko; 6108 ft.

Ho–t'ien \'hō-'tyen\ *also* **Kho·tan** \'kō-'tän\. 1 River, W Sinkiang Uighur, W China; joins the Yarkand to form Tarim river, but dry much of the year.
2 Town, China. See KHOTAN 2.

Hotin. See KHOTIN.

Hot Spring. County in Arkansas. See table at ARKANSAS.

Hot Springs. 1 County in Wyoming. See table at WYOMING.
2 City, ⊗ of Garland co., W cen. Arkansas, in Ouachita Mts. 47 m. WSW of Little Rock; pop. (1970c) 35,631; health and tourist resort noted for its 47 thermal springs. Settled 1807; made, with surrounding area, a U.S. Government reservation 1832, **Hot Springs National Park** 1921 (see UNITED STATES, *National Parks*).
3 City, New Mexico. See TRUTH OR CONSEQUENCES.
4 City, ⊗ of Fall River co., SW corner of South Dakota, in foothills of Black Hills 48 m. S of Rapid City; pop. (1970c) 4434; health resort; thermal and mineral springs; sandstone quarries; mica, feldspar, gold, silver mines.
5 Village, Bath co., W Virginia, 5 m. SW of Warm Springs; mineral springs; Japanese diplomats interned here 1942 at beginning of war with Japan; scene of United Nations Conference on Food and Agriculture 1943.

Hot Springs Peak. Mountain, Humboldt co., NW Nevada; 6450 ft.

Hot Sul·phur Springs \-'səl-fər-\. Town, ⊗ of Grand co., N Colorado; pop. (1970c) 220; hot sulfur springs.

Hotte, Massif de la. See SUD, MASSIF DU.

Hot·ten·tot Point \ˌhät-ᵊn-ˌtät-\. Cape on SW coast of South-West Africa, N of Lüderitz.

Hou·dain \ü-'daⁿ\. Commune, Pas-de-Calais dept., N France, near Béthune; pop. (1962c) 8869; coal; has church (12th and 16th cents.); destroyed in World War I and rebuilt.

Hou·dan \ü-'däⁿ\. Village, Yvelines dept., N France; pop. (1962c) 2358; has 15th–16th cent. church and keep of an early 12th cent. castle; noted for its poultry market, the Houdan breed of domestic fowl originating here.

Hou·deng–Goe·gnies \ü-ˌdäⁿ-gər-'nyē\. Commune, Hainaut prov., SW Belgium, on a tributary of the Haine, E of Mons; pop. (1969e) 8947; coal mines, smelting, woodworking, rope making, glassworks.

Houf·fa·lize \ˌü-fə-'lēz\. Village, Luxembourg prov., SE Belgium, 10 m. N of Bastogne; pop. (1969e) 1346; taken by Germans in ... ly phase ... le of the Bulge Dec. 1944;

Geographical dictionaries, or *gazetteers*, are made up of alphabetical lists of geographic names. General gazetteers list all kinds of geographical features—including countries, cities, counties, landforms, bodies of water, and more—each followed by a brief description. The description usually tells the size and location of a feature, as well as how to pronounce its name. Gazetteers often define the location of a place by latitude and longitude coordinates, or by the number of miles it is from a well-known location.

Almanacs, unlike geographical dictionaries, are not organized alphabetically. Instead, they have detailed indexes to help you locate geographic information.

New Jersey (see States, U.S.)	
Admission, area, capital	386,640
Agriculture	160,161,162,163
Altitudes (high, low)	385
Birth, death statistics	939
Bridges	622-624
Budget	154
Chamber of Commerce	640
Commerce at ports	674
Congressmen	74,579,583
Courts, U.S.	596
Debt	154
Ethnic, racial distribution	640
Fair	640
Geographic center	387
Governors	598,601
Income, per capita	640
Interest, laws, rates	713
Marriages, divorce laws	722-723,942
Name, origin of	388
Population	129

Parts of a Map

Elevation means the height of land above sea level. It is shown on maps using contour lines. Elevation can also be shown using shading or colors.

The **directional arrow** shows the directions—north, south, east, and west, and sometimes northwest, northeast, southeast, and southwest—in relation to the map. These directions show the orientation of the map. Most world maps show north on the top and south on the bottom, east to the right, and west to the left. Maps of smaller areas often use this standard orientation, too. Some directional arrows are plain and simple. Others are decorated.

A **compass rose** is an ornamental directional arrow often used on ship charts and old-fashioned maps. The rose is usually drawn from a circle divided into 360 degrees, and is used to tell directions from magnetic north, or 0 degrees (0°) on the compass.

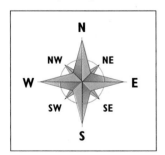

A map **index** is included on some maps. It is a list of place-names, complete with coordinates for finding the places on the map.

Symbols, or **icons**, are used on maps to represent real objects or places. Symbols can be simple dots to indicate cities, pictographs (tiny pictures) to indicate products, or colors to show location. Symbols are explained in the map key or legend.

Major Cities

Bologna	D-2
Firenza	D-2
Genova	C-2
Milano	C-1
Palermo	E-4
Roma	E-3
Venezia	D-1

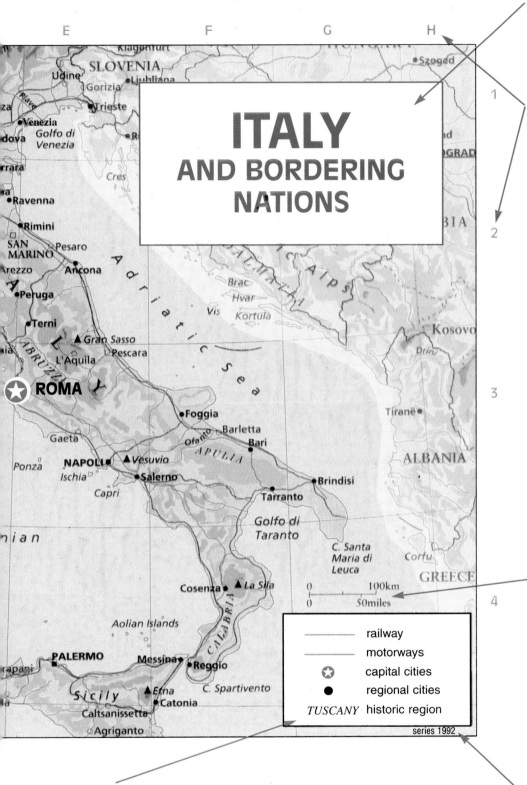

A **title** is included to tell map readers what the map is about.

Coordinates are a set of points or spaces, for example, *G-2*, located by using the map grid. The map index uses a map grid to help the reader find a specific location.

A **map grid** is a grid drawn on a map. You can read the map grid by looking in the margins of the map. The letters *A*, *B*, *C*, etc., run along the top and bottom margins. The numbers *1*, *2*, *3*, etc., run along the left and right margins. If a place is identified at *D–3*, simply find the square on the grid where column *D* and row *3* intersect. The map grid may or may not follow the geographic grid of latitude and longitude. Many highway maps have their own grids.

The map **scale** shows how the size of the map relates to the size of a real place. It may be stated in words, in combinations of words and numbers, and in ratios. For example, if a map's scale is 1 inch=100 miles, one inch on the map represents one hundred miles in the real world.

A **key** or **legend** lists the symbols used on a map and tells what each symbol means. For example, on some maps, cities can be represented by different sized dots. Large dots can stand for large cities and small dots for small cities or towns. Maps and keys are usually set apart from the rest of a map, often in a box.

Dates appear on many maps to tell when the map was drawn.

Understanding and Comparing Maps

To understand a map, you must be able to "read" it.

Once you can read maps, you can compare maps. By comparing the information on different maps, you can learn how many features work together to make a place special. For example, if you compare a map of North American waterways to a map of North American cities, you'll find that most cities are located on waterways. This is important geographical information—it shows that water is one thing people think about when deciding where to live.

Three Steps to Reading Maps

1 Look at the map title. It will tell you what type of information, as well as which region or location, is shown on the map.

2 Look at the map scale. Some maps are very simple. Others show a lot of detail. The amount and type of detail on a map depend on the map scale, or the size of the area shown on the map. For example, it would be difficult to show the location of houses on a map of your state. However, it would be a logical feature on a map of your neighborhood. Successfully reading a map means understanding its scale.

3 Look at the legend. The legend will tell you what the symbols on the map mean. In order to understand the map fully, you will need to understand the symbols and the type of information they convey.

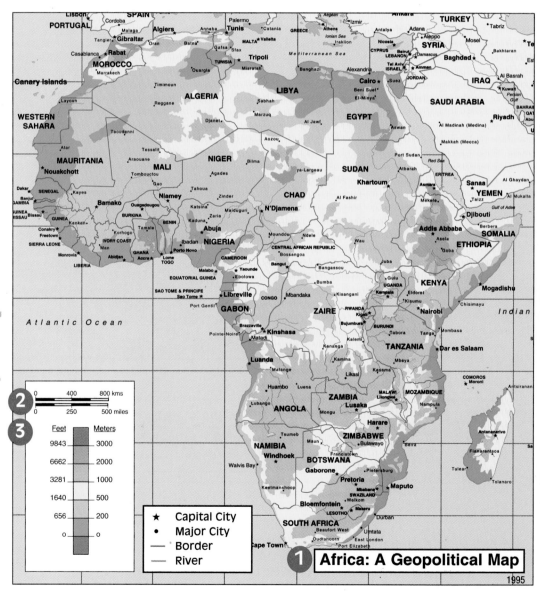

Africa: A Geopolitical Map

28

Three Steps to Comparing Maps

1 Choose maps that show information you want to compare.

2 Locate your area of interest on both maps.

3 Use the map symbols to read both maps. Then note how the maps are alike and how they are different. When you are using two or more maps, watch for map scale, the type of projections used (see p. 17), and the date the maps were published.

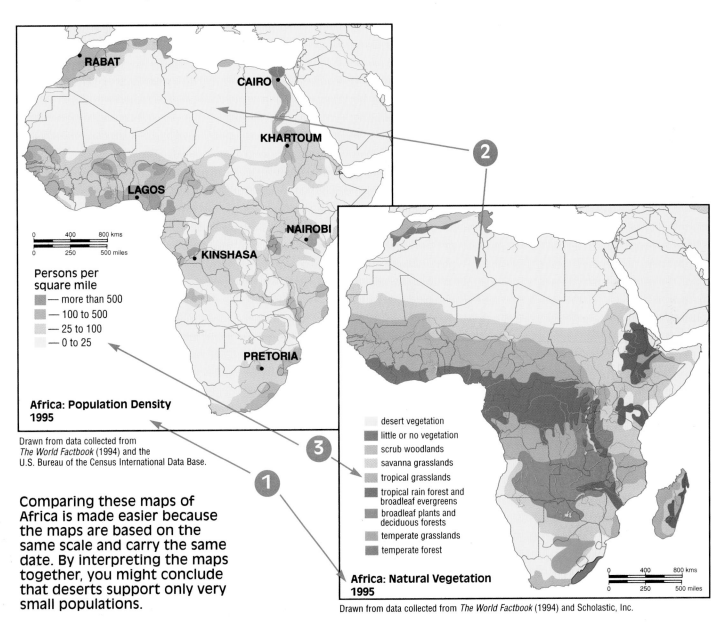

Africa: Population Density 1995

Persons per square mile
- — more than 500
- — 100 to 500
- — 25 to 100
- — 0 to 25

Drawn from data collected from *The World Factbook* (1994) and the U.S. Bureau of the Census International Data Base.

Africa: Natural Vegetation 1995

- desert vegetation
- little or no vegetation
- scrub woodlands
- savanna grasslands
- tropical grasslands
- tropical rain forest and broadleaf evergreens
- broadleaf plants and deciduous forests
- temperate grasslands
- temperate forest

Drawn from data collected from *The World Factbook* (1994) and Scholastic, Inc.

Comparing these maps of Africa is made easier because the maps are based on the same scale and carry the same date. By interpreting the maps together, you might conclude that deserts support only very small populations.

LAND, WATER, AND AIR: THE PHYSICAL WORLD

1 The Land

How the Earth Was Formed

Geographers believe that about 4.6 billion years ago a cloud of dust particles came together to form a ball of melted rock. The ball cooled over several million years, forming the earth.

As the molten rock ball cooled, a thin solid layer formed over the surface of the earth. This layer is called the **crust**. The crust is about 2 miles thick under the deepest parts of the ocean and up to 75 miles thick under the tallest mountain peaks.

The earth's **core** has two parts: the **outer core** and the **inner core**. The outer core is made up of molten rock. The inner core is solid. The core has a radius of about 2,100 miles.

The **mantle** lies between the earth's crust and core. It is a layer of very hot, sometimes melted rock about 1,800 miles thick.

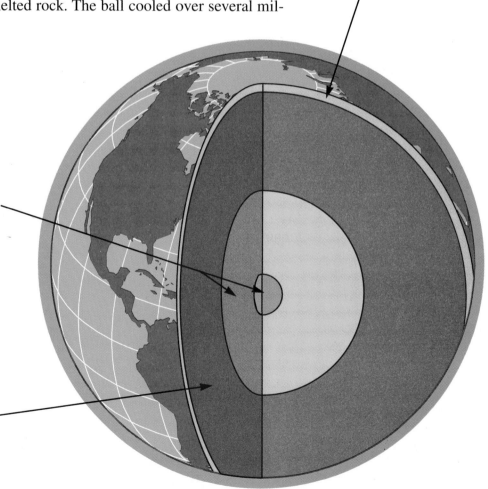

Plate Tectonics

Continents are the large landmasses on earth: Africa, Australia, Antarctica, North America, South America, and Eurasia. Eurasia is sometimes considered two continents, divided by the Ural Mountains and the Caspian Sea into Europe to the west and Asia to the east.

The crust of the earth is not one solid piece. It is broken into large pieces, called ***tectonic plates***. The plates are like enormous ships that float upon the earth's mantle.

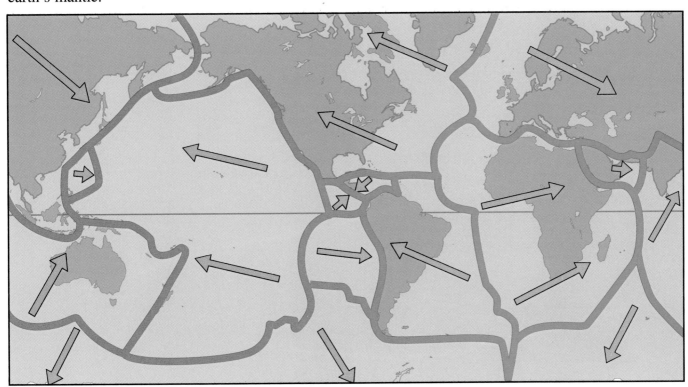

World map showing fault lines and the direction of tectonic plate movement.

Fault Lines

Fault lines occur along the edges where tectonic plates meet. As the plates move, a number of tectonic events occur along the fault lines.

Pangaea and Continental Drift

Scientists believe that about 200 million years ago, all the continents were connected. They formed a supercontinent that scientists call ***Pangaea***.

Then the continents separated at places where the tectonic plates broke apart. Like ships on water, the plates slowly moved apart, and the continents we know today were formed.

The continents are still moving. This movement is called ***continental drift***. In another 200 million years, the continents may be connected again or may have drifted into a completely different arrangement on the planet.

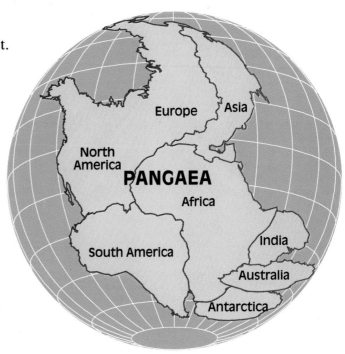

Tectonic Events That Shape the Land

Tectonic plates are moving in different directions at different speeds. The features on the surface of the earth tell us where the plates push beneath each other or collide.

Mountains

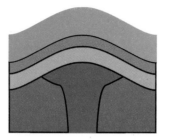

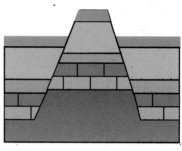

Most **volcanoes** form when molten rock from deep inside the earth rises to the surface at or near a fault line or a soft spot in a plate. The molten rock spurts out of the top of the volcano in the form of lava.

Dome mountains form when molten rock pushes up toward the earth's surface along a fault line but doesn't break through the surface of the earth.

Block mountains form when blocks of rock split along fault lines and slide in opposite directions.

Fold mountains form when tectonic plates move against each other and push and squeeze up the crust of the earth.

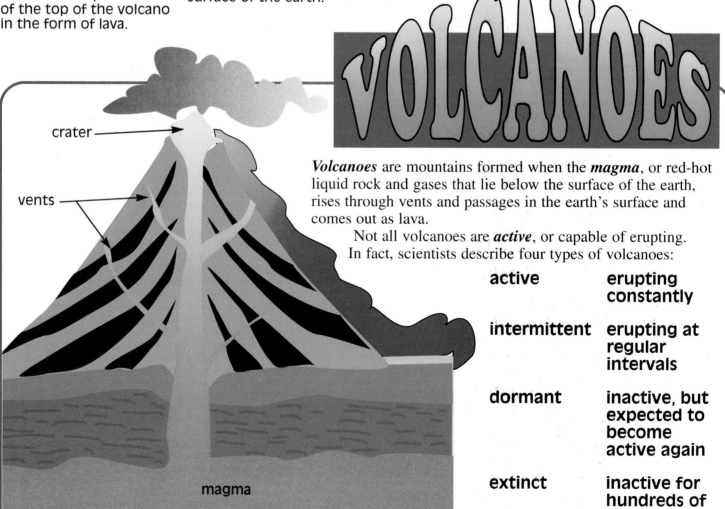

crater

vents

magma

VOLCANOES

Volcanoes are mountains formed when the *magma*, or red-hot liquid rock and gases that lie below the surface of the earth, rises through vents and passages in the earth's surface and comes out as lava.

Not all volcanoes are *active*, or capable of erupting. In fact, scientists describe four types of volcanoes:

active	**erupting constantly**
intermittent	**erupting at regular intervals**
dormant	**inactive, but expected to become active again**
extinct	**inactive for hundreds of years**

Earthquakes

Earthquakes are sudden shifting movements in the earth's surface. Some earthquakes cannot even be felt, yet others are strong enough to knock down skyscrapers and twist highways as if they were ribbons.

Earthquakes happen when tectonic plates collide, separate, or scrape against one another along fault lines.

1

Forces push tectonic plates into one another, causing them to collide or scrape against each other.

2

Over thousands of years, the forces cause the rocks along the fault line to bend and twist.

3

Finally, the force becomes so great that the rocks break loose and jolt past each other, causing an earthquake.

THE RING OF FIRE

Where Volcanoes and Earthquakes Often Happen

Volcanoes and earthquakes most frequently occur along the fault lines in the earth's tectonic plates. The Ring of Fire in the Pacific Ocean is the world's most active area of earthquake and volcanic activity. Why? The faults in the Atlantic are, for the most part, expanding, or moving away from each other. But in the Pacific, the the plates are colliding, or rubbing up against each other (see above, also p. 31).

Landforms

Landforms are the natural features of the earth's land surface, including mountains, other highlands, plains, and lowlands.

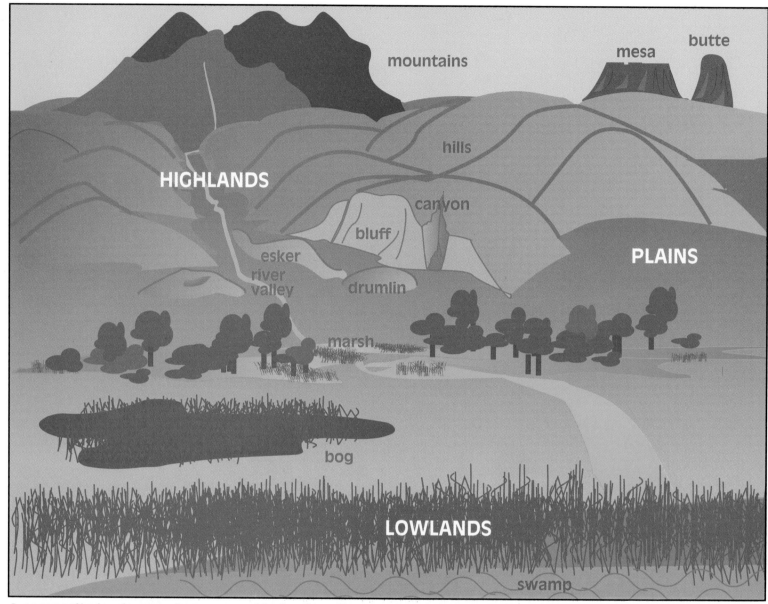

A composite landscape shows many kinds of landforms. (For definitions of the specific landforms, see Glossary pp. 88–99.)

Mountains and High Land

A *mountain* is any point on land that rises quickly to at least 1,000 feet above its surroundings. Some mountains are jagged and snowcapped, others are rounded and smooth. Some are volcanoes, with large craters in their tops.

Mountains exist, too, below the oceans. Some of these mountains, while deep under the salty water, rise even higher than Mount Everest, the highest mountain on the continents.

A *hill* is an area on the earth's surface that rises above the land, but not more than 1,000 feet above the surrounding area. Any high land that is not a mountain can be classified as a hill. However, geologists and geographers have developed a special vocabulary for high landforms based on how the landforms were created.

Plains

Plains are large, flat, mostly treeless areas of land.

Lowlands

A *lowland* is an area of land that is lower than the land surrounding it. Just as geologists and geographers have a special vocabulary for highlands, they have a special vocabulary for lowlands.

A *valley* is a natural low place in the earth's surface, often located between mountains or hills. The bottom of a valley is called its *floor*, the sides its *walls*. A ridge between valleys is called a *divide*. Valleys with steep cliff walls are called *canyons* or *gorges*.

Other natural lowlands are *wetlands*, where the water level stays at or above the land's surface for most of the year. *Bogs, marshes,* and *swamps* are the most common types of wetlands.

Erosion and Weathering

Erosion is the gradual wearing away of land by the action of wind, water, or glaciers. *Weathering* is the gradual breakdown of rocks by weather, including wind, rain, snow, and changes in temperature (see p. 44). Erosion and weathering work together constantly to change the landforms on Earth.

Water running over gentle slopes takes earth with it as it moves from a large area. This process is called sheet erosion.

When water runs rapidly downhill, it carves gullies in the land, taking with it large amounts of dirt and rock. This process is called gully or rill erosion.

Rivers and streams are the great movers of earth. When rivers run into lakes or oceans, they dump tons of dirt that they have carried for long distances. This dirt is called silt when it is deposited in standing water.

The wind blows dirt from the surface of the land when it is not protected with a covering of vegetation.

 The study of the earth's physical features is called geomorphology.

Glaciers

Glaciers are slow-moving sheets of ice found in high mountain valleys and polar regions. Glaciers cover about six million square miles, or three percent of the earth's surface.

Glaciers form at high latitudes and high elevations, where it is cold enough that more snow falls than melts or evaporates. Over the years, the snow gets deeper and deeper. Pressure from the weight of the snow finally turns the snow into huge sheets of ice. These ice sheets flow, like slow-moving rivers, down mountainsides until they reach warmer air along the oceans or at lower elevations. There the ice sheets melt or break off to form floating *icebergs*.

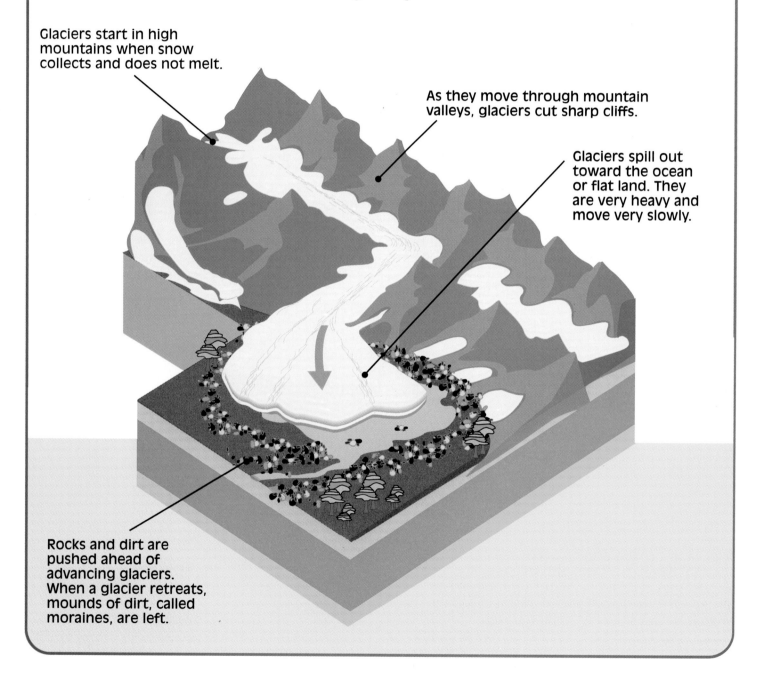

Glaciers start in high mountains when snow collects and does not melt.

As they move through mountain valleys, glaciers cut sharp cliffs.

Glaciers spill out toward the ocean or flat land. They are very heavy and move very slowly.

Rocks and dirt are pushed ahead of advancing glaciers. When a glacier retreats, mounds of dirt, called moraines, are left.

2 The Water

Oceans

Oceans are large bodies of salt water that cover almost three-fourths of the earth's surface.

Atlantic Ocean

covers 33,420,000 square miles at an average depth of 11,700 feet

Arctic Ocean

covers 5,120,000 square miles at an average depth of 3,400 feet

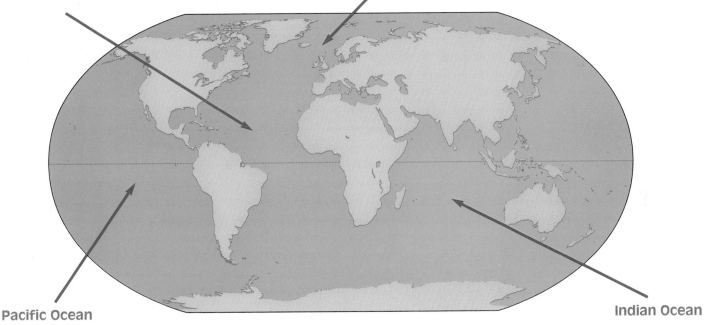

Pacific Ocean

covers 64,200,000 square miles at an average depth of 12,900 feet

Indian Ocean

covers 28,400,000 square miles at an average depth 12,600 feet

THE BRINY DEEP

	Depth (Feet)	Depth (Meters)		Depth (Feet)	Depth (Meters)
Pacific Ocean			**Indian Ocean**		
Mariana Trench	35,800	10,900	Java Trench	23,400	7,100
Tonga Trench	35,400	10,800	Ob' Trench	22,600	6,900
Philippine Trench	33,000	10,000	Diamantina Trench	21,700	6,600
Kermadec Trench	33,000	10,000	Vema Trench	21,000	6,400
Atlantic Ocean			**Arctic Ocean**		
Puerto Rico Trench	28,200	8,600	Eurasia Basin	17,900	5,500
South Sandwich Trench	27,300	8,300	**Mediterranean Sea**		
Cayman Trench	24,700	7,500	Ionian Basin	16,900	5,200
Romanche Gap	24,400	7,700			

The ocean floor, like the surface of the land, is made up of many features. Huge trenches drop off deeply from underwater plains. Plateaus and ridges rise thousands of feet to form mountains on the ocean floor. As on the land, the underwater surface is formed by the movements of tectonic plates and shaped by the movement of water (see p. 31 and below).

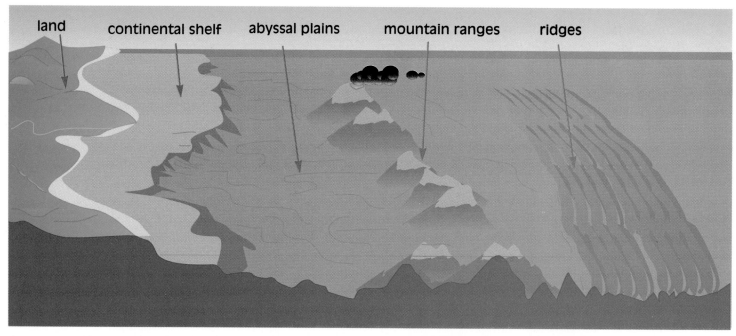

land   continental shelf   abyssal plains   mountain ranges   ridges

A cross section of the ocean floor shows some of the many features of its landscape.

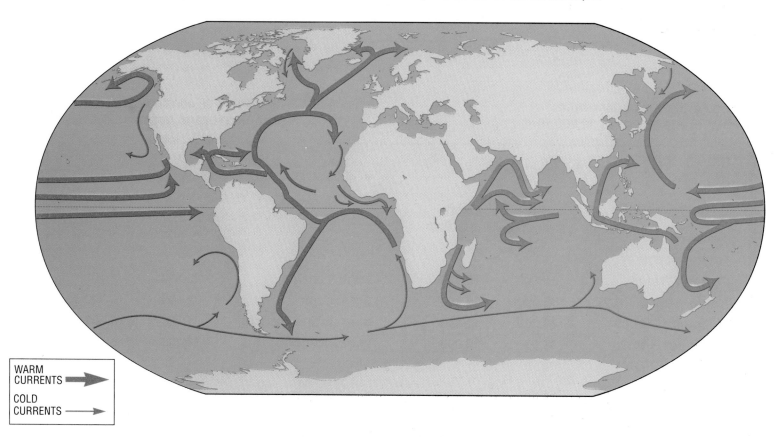

WARM CURRENTS
COLD CURRENTS

Ocean currents flow in predictable patterns throughout the major water bodies of the earth.

Natural Events Under Water

As on land, erosion, earthquakes, and volcanoes make regular changes under water.

In addition to changing the ocean floor, underwater volcanoes and earthquakes cause giant surges of water in the ocean. These surges of water aren't noticeable at sea, but when they near shore, they can rise anywhere from six to sixty feet high. When the surge of water, called a *tsunami*, hits land, it can cause dangerous flooding and wash away homes, roads, and buildings in its path.

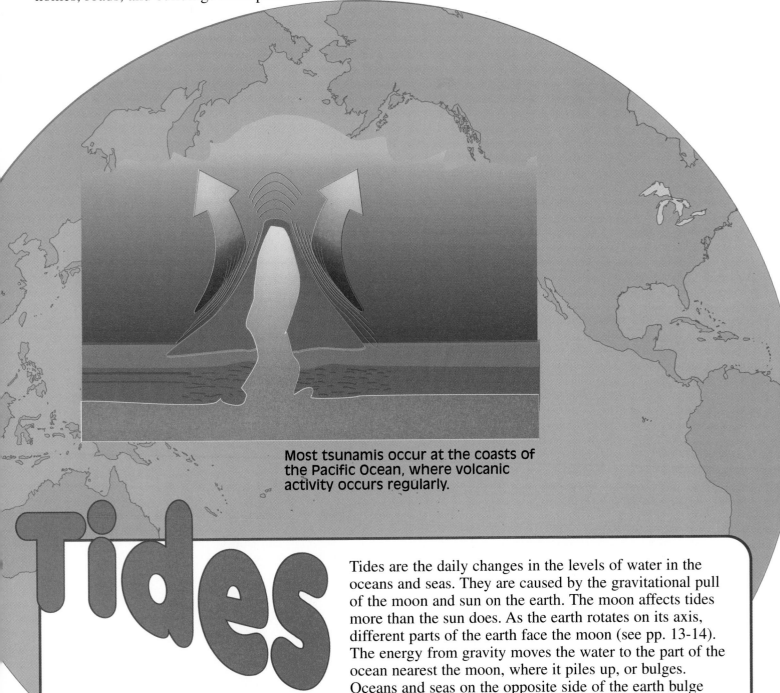

Most tsunamis occur at the coasts of the Pacific Ocean, where volcanic activity occurs regularly.

Tides

Tides are the daily changes in the levels of water in the oceans and seas. They are caused by the gravitational pull of the moon and sun on the earth. The moon affects tides more than the sun does. As the earth rotates on its axis, different parts of the earth face the moon (see pp. 13-14). The energy from gravity moves the water to the part of the ocean nearest the moon, where it piles up, or bulges. Oceans and seas on the opposite side of the earth bulge because of the way the earth spins. The bulges of water travel around the earth from east to west. They bring high tides to ocean and seashores every 12 hours. When the bulge reaches a shore, it is high tide. When it is away from the shore, it is low tide.

Rivers

Rivers are bodies of water than begin at a source and flow downhill between *banks* of earth to a *mouth*, where they empty into a larger body of water. Most large rivers have three parts, or *courses: upper, middle,* and *estuary*.

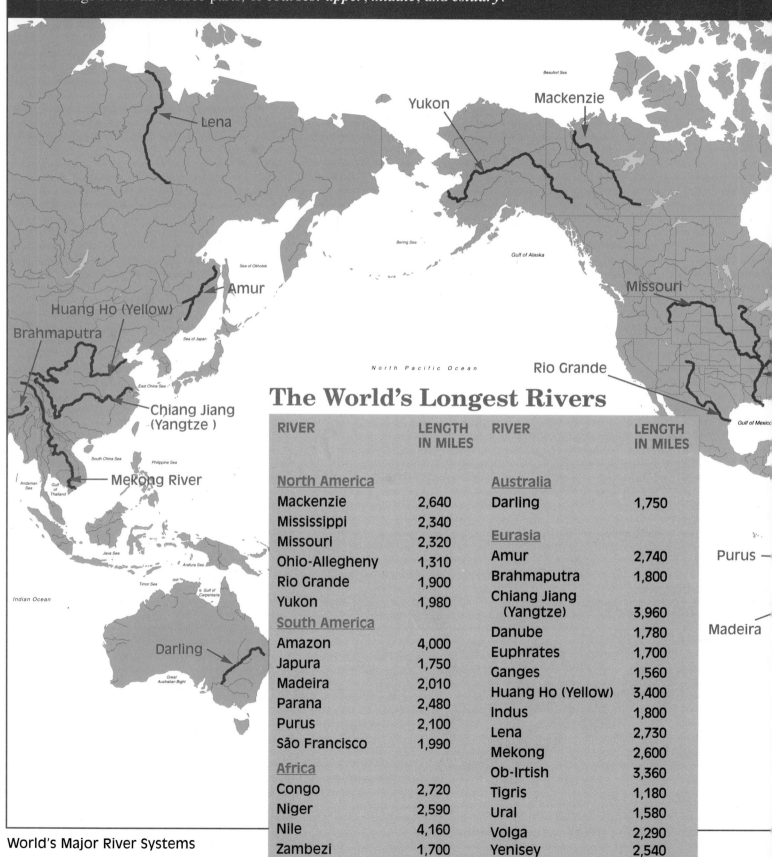

The World's Longest Rivers

RIVER	LENGTH IN MILES	RIVER	LENGTH IN MILES
North America		**Australia**	
Mackenzie	2,640	Darling	1,750
Mississippi	2,340		
Missouri	2,320	**Eurasia**	
Ohio-Allegheny	1,310	Amur	2,740
Rio Grande	1,900	Brahmaputra	1,800
Yukon	1,980	Chiang Jiang (Yangtze)	3,960
South America		Danube	1,780
Amazon	4,000	Euphrates	1,700
Japura	1,750	Ganges	1,560
Madeira	2,010	Huang Ho (Yellow)	3,400
Parana	2,480	Indus	1,800
Purus	2,100	Lena	2,730
São Francisco	1,990	Mekong	2,600
Africa		Ob-Irtish	3,360
Congo	2,720	Tigris	1,180
Niger	2,590	Ural	1,580
Nile	4,160	Volga	2,290
Zambezi	1,700	Yenisey	2,540

World's Major River Systems

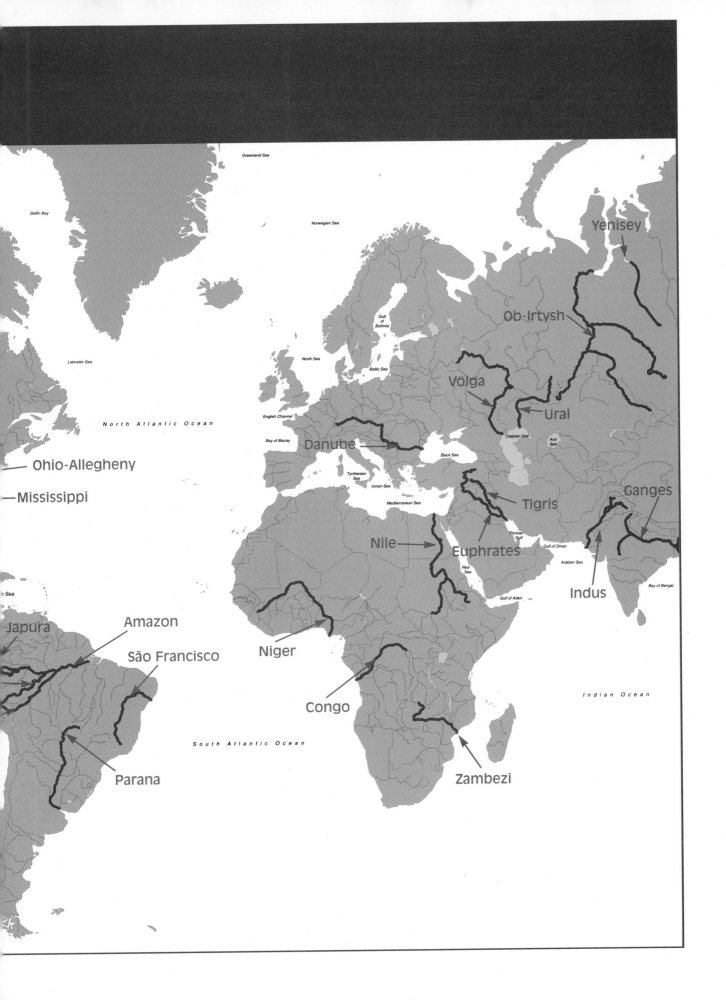

Ohio-Allegheny

Mississippi

Japura

Amazon

São Francisco

Niger

Parana

Congo

Zambezi

Danube

Volga

Ob-Irtysh

Yenisey

Ural

Nile

Tigris

Euphrates

Ganges

Indus

Parts of a River

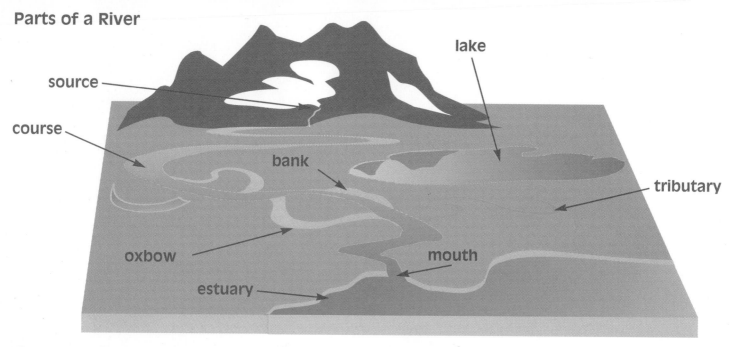

The source of the river shown here is melted water from a glacier, although rivers also form from the waters of highland springs and lakes flowing downhill, and from a combination of these waters. All rivers flow from a source to a mouth, where river waters empty into a larger body of water, sometimes another river, or a bay, gulf, lake, sea, or ocean. (For definitions of specific river parts, see Glossary, pp. 88-99.)

Seas, Gulfs, and Bays

Seas are large bodies of salt or fresh water that are partly or completely enclosed by land. *Gulfs* and *bays* are large bodies of ocean or sea water that are partly surrounded by land. Bays are usually smaller than gulfs.

Lakes

Lakes are natural and human-made low spots on the land that have filled with water from flooding, melting glacial ice, rivers, and groundwater traveling downhill.

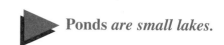 *Most lakes hold fresh water, although some hold salt water.*

Ponds are small lakes.

Four Kinds of Lakes

Lakes can be divided into four types, depending on how they are formed.

Crater Lake

Water collects in craters left by volcanoes.

Glacial Lake

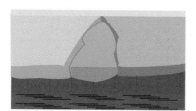

Ice from glaciers carves depressions (low areas) in the landscape. The ice melts and forms a lake.

Rift Valley Lake

Shifts in plates on the earth's surface form depressions that fill with water.

Artificial Lake

Lakes are created artificially by building dams on rivers or by digging depressions and filling them with water from nearby sources.

3 The Air: Atmosphere, Weather, and Climate

The Atmosphere

The *atmosphere* is the air that surrounds the earth. It is made up of five main layers. Although we don't pay much attention to the atmosphere most of the time, it is taller than any mountain, it extends past the horizon, and it is a very important element in the earth's geography. Without the atmosphere, the many variations in weather and climate that we know on the earth would not occur, and without those variations, different natural regions would not exist (see p. 50). Also, weather and climate affect the landforms physically through the processes of erosion and weathering (see p. 35).

Exosphere

The border between the earth and space at about 310 miles. Satellites revolve around the earth in the exosphere.

Mesosphere

Ranges to about 50 miles. Temperatures drop to under -100°F.

Stratosphere

Stretches to about 30 miles. Icy winds blow through the lower parts, speeding supersonic jets like the Concorde to their destinations. Above the clouds, the air is usually dry and clear. The ozone layer, which absorbs harmful ultraviolet rays from the sun, is here.

Thermosphere

Ranges to about 400 miles above the earth's surface. Within the thermosphere, electrically charged particles called ions make up the ionosphere. Radio waves beamed up through the atmosphere bounce back to earth from the ion layers.

Troposphere

About 12 miles thick at the equator and 5 miles thick at the poles. More than half the atmosphere's gases, water vapor, and dust particles are in the first 4 miles. We live here. Clouds and weather form here, too.

43

Weather and Climate

Weather is the day-to-day change in the atmosphere around us. The weather in a place varies constantly. It can be sunny and warm one day, cool and cloudy the next. Some days it rains, others it snows. Although many elements make up weather, two of the most important are temperature and precipitation (rain, snow, sleet, hail, or drizzle). The third most important element is wind.

Climate is the usual weather in an area over a long period of time. Some words that describe different climates are tropical, temperate, and arctic. (See also Biomes, pp. 51-56).

Heat

Most of the heat on Earth comes from the sun. (The rest radiates outward from the very hot interior of the earth.) The heat from the sun begins as sunlight passing through the atmosphere and being absorbed into the earth. It then changes to heat and rises from the surface of the earth to warm the atmosphere. This warming of the atmosphere near the earth's surface helps create wind systems and the patterns of weather.

The most important cause of weather is heat in the atmosphere. But not all sunlight that enters the earth's atmosphere is converted to heat. Some of the light is reflected back into space from the white tops of clouds and tiny particles of ice and water in the atmosphere. Some of the light reaches the surface of the earth and reflects off snow, water, and other reflective surfaces. Plants with green leaves absorb some of the light and change it into sugar and starch in the process called *photosynthesis*. The rest of the light is absorbed into the earth, converted into heat, and radiated back into the atmosphere, where its rising and cooling help create wind and weather.

Air Pressure

The weight of the atmosphere pressing down on the earth is called *air pressure*. Because warm air is less dense than cold air, warm air forms areas of low air pressure and cold air forms areas of high pressure. High pressure usually means clear skies and sunny weather. Low pressure usually means cloudy, rainy (or snowy) weather.

Dalol, Ethiopia, has the highest annual average temperature on Earth— 94°F. Nedostupnosti Polyus, Antarctica, has the coldest annual average temperature— -72°F. Nedostupnosti Polyus means "inaccessible pole."

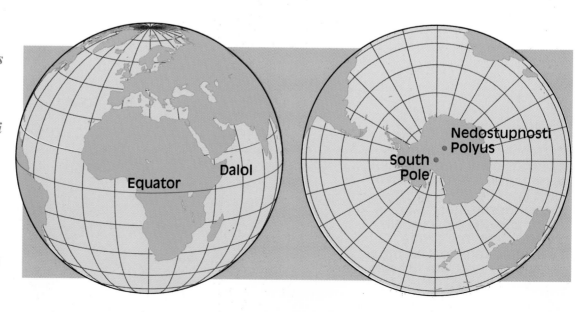

Weather Fronts

Cold Front

Cold air moves in on an area of warm air. The heavier cold air slides in underneath the lighter warm air mass and pushes it up. ***Clouds*** and ***thunderstorms*** often form.

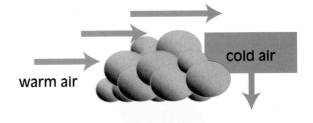

Warm Front

Warm air moves in on an area of cold air. The lighter warm air slides over the heavy, cold air, creating a front with a gentle slope. Clouds form, usually leading to some form of ***precipitation.***

Stationary Front

Cold and warm air masses meet, but neither moves on the other. Clouds often form at the boundary.

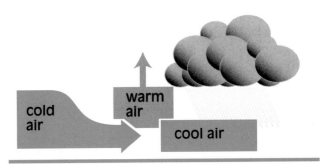

Occluded Fronts

When warm air is trapped between cold and cool air, it is forced upward. Clouds and precipitation usually result.

In places where the sun's rays reach the earth most directly and for the longest periods of time, the climate is warmer than in other places. Likewise, the coldest places are located where the sun's rays reach the earth less directly and for shorter periods of time.

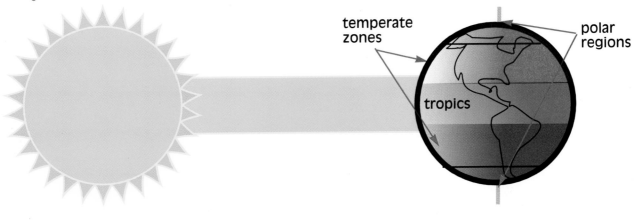

Water Heaters:
Land and Ocean Temperatures

Oceans heat up more slowly than landmasses. They also cool down more slowly. That means that in the summer the ocean is cooler than the land. It cools the air above it. This cool ocean air moves across the coastal land, keeping it cool. In winter, the water is warmer than the land, so the ocean air helps warm the air over coastal land. Temperatures vary less from summer to winter near oceans than they do in the middle of continents.

In summer, the cooler water cools the air that moves from the sea to the coast.

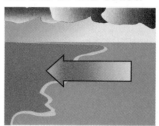

In winter, the warmer water warms the air that moves from the sea to the coast.

Air

When air moves between areas of high and low pressure, **wind** results. The greater the difference in the pressure, the greater the speed of the wind. But air doesn't move in a straight line from one area to another. Instead, winds circle areas of high and low pressure, moving in opposite directions.

Warm air rises at the equator, and winds move in from north and south to take its place. The warm air cools and falls at around 30 degrees of latitude north and south, returning to the equator to replace other rising air. This circulation helps to cause similar air movements between 30 and 60 degrees latitude and between 60 degrees and the poles. The winds do not blow directly north and south because Earth's rotation skews them at an angle.

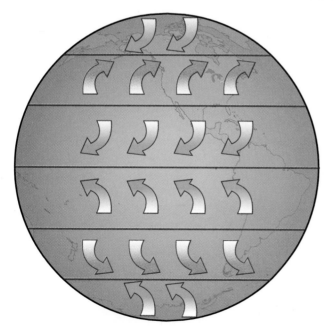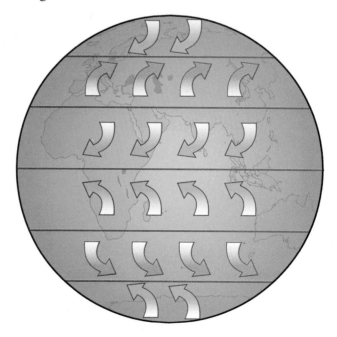

Prevailing wind patterns around the earth.

HURRICANES, TORNADOES, TYPHOONS, AND CYCLONES

Hurricanes, tornadoes, typhoon, and cyclones are spirals of air moving around areas of intense low pressure.

Tornadoes are small, tightly spiraling storms that occur over land, most often forming over the Great Plains and in the upper midwest of the United States from late spring until fall. They also occur infrequently in many other parts of the world.

Hurricanes, typhoons, and *cyclones* are three names for large spiraling storms that form over water and then sometimes move onto land, causing great damage. They can topple trees and lift houses off their foundations. When these storms occur in the North Atlantic Ocean, Caribbean Sea, Gulf of Mexico, or in the eastern North Pacific near Mexico and Central America, they are called hurricanes. When they occur in the North Pacific, west of the International Date Line, near China, Japan, and Southeast Asia, they are called typhoons. When they occur in the South Pacific or the India Ocean, they are called cyclones.

The word *cyclone* also means any circling air, from fast-moving, tiny dust devils to slow-moving, thousand-mile-wide areas of low pressure, so tornadoes, hurricanes, and typhoons are all sometimes called cyclones.

- Typhoons
- Hurricanes
- Tornadoes
- Cyclones

Water in the Air

Water and heat work together to create different weather conditions. Heat warms water in lakes, rivers, and oceans. The water *evaporates*, or changes from liquid to a gas called *water vapor*. Water vapor cools and condenses into droplets in the atmosphere to form clouds, fog, or ice crystals. These droplets grow heavier and fall back to the earth in the form of precipitation—rain, snow, sleet, hail, or drizzle. Warm air can hold more water vapor than cold air. That means that the humidity—or the amount of water vapor in the air—is usually greater on warm days than on cold ones.

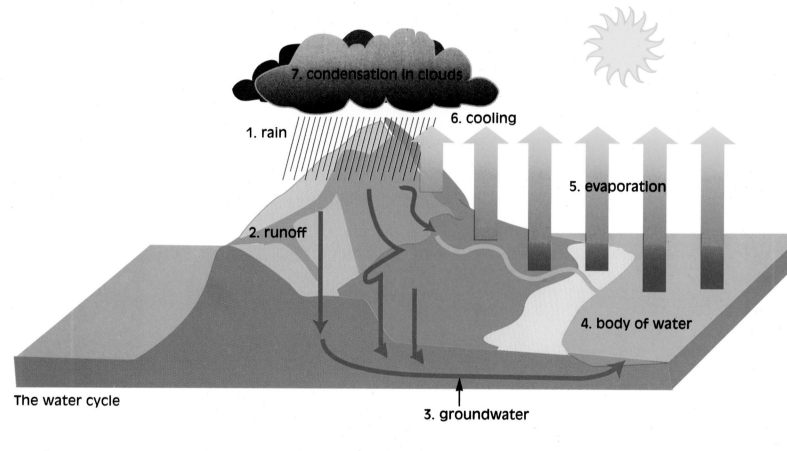

The water cycle

 On any day, about four trillion (4,000,000,000,000) gallons of water—about ten times the amount of water in all the world's rivers—are in the atmosphere in the form of water vapor.

 The amount of moisture in the air is called **humidity**. *Humidity is referred to in percentages. For example, when the air is completely filled with water vapor, the humidity is 100 percent. When the air is holding about half the water vapor it can hold, the humidity is measured at 50 percent.*

48

INSULATION: CLOUDS AND CLIMATE

Insulation prevents heat from passing into or out of an area. Your coat insulates your body, keeping your body heat in. The thick walls of a refrigerator keep the cold air inside and prevent the warm air outside from getting in.

   Clouds insulate the earth. During the day they act as shields reflecting the sun's light and keep much of it from reaching the surface of the earth. At night, they act as blankets reflecting heat leaving the earth's surface downward again. So cloudy skies tend to bring smaller swings of temperature from day to night than clear skies.

Winds at Sea

The warm and cold winds that blow across the earth don't just move air. They also push surface water along as waves. These become ocean currents, some warm and others cold. Warm and cold currents, like winds, affect the weather and climate in different places on the earth. (See also ocean currents map, p. 38.)

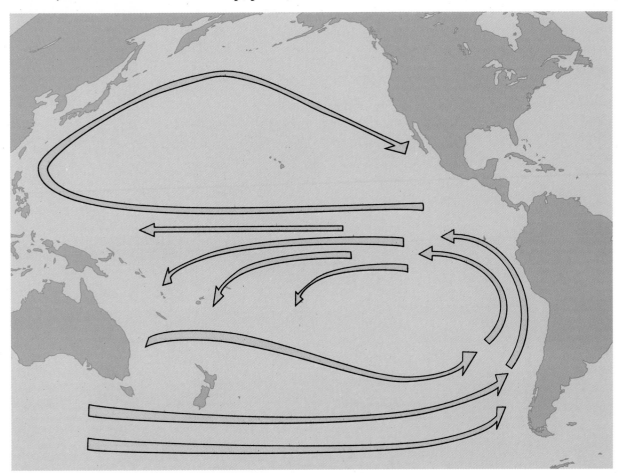

This map shows the pattern of winds over the Pacific Ocean.

PLANTS AND ANIMALS

1 The Natural Regions of the World

Land Biomes

The earth can be divided into about ten different natural regions, or *land biomes*. Each biome is unique, with a special mixture of physical features—landforms, bodies of water, and climate—and their own forms of plant and animal life.

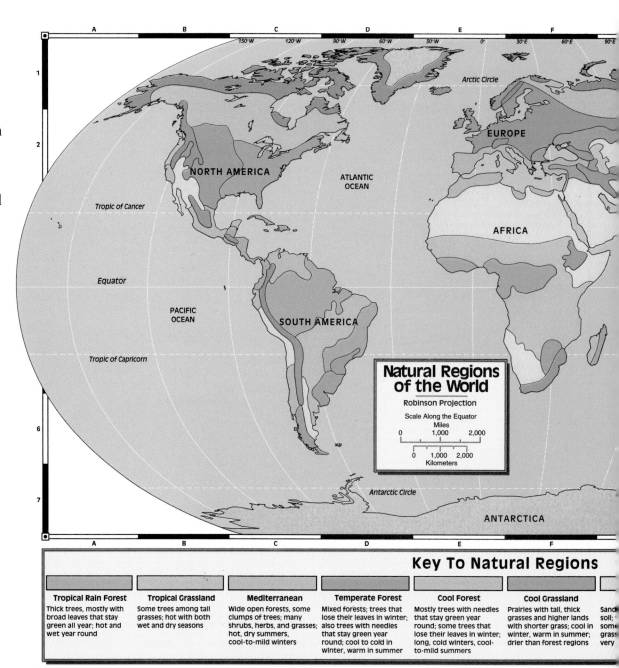

Natural Regions of the World

Robinson Projection

Scale Along the Equator
Miles
0   1,000   2,000

0 1,000 2,000
Kilometers

Arctic Circle

EUROPE

NORTH AMERICA

ATLANTIC OCEAN

Tropic of Cancer

AFRICA

Equator

PACIFIC OCEAN

SOUTH AMERICA

Tropic of Capricorn

Antarctic Circle

ANTARCTICA

Key To Natural Regions

Tropical Rain Forest
Thick trees, mostly with broad leaves that stay green all year; hot and wet year round

Tropical Grassland
Some trees among tall grasses; hot with both wet and dry seasons

Mediterranean
Wide open forests, some clumps of trees; many shrubs, herbs, and grasses; hot, dry summers, cool-to-mild winters

Temperate Forest
Mixed forests; trees that lose their leaves in winter; also trees with needles that stay green year round; cool to cold in winter, warm in summer

Cool Forest
Mostly trees with needles that stay green year round; some trees that lose their leaves in winter; long, cold winters, cool-to-mild summers

Cool Grassland
Prairies among tall, thick grasses and higher lands with shorter grass; cool in winter, warm in summer; drier than forest regions

50

2 The Biomes

Tropical Rain Forests

Tropical rain forests are warm, wet biomes near or at the equator, where more species of plants and animals flourish than in all other biomes combined.

Hundreds of varieties of trees grow in tropical rain forests, most of them hardwoods. Although the warm, wet conditions encourage luxurious growth, the trees grow so close together that they have to fight for the light they need to grow. To catch more light, trees grow very tall, and the upper branches spread out over a wide area. The tops of trees grow close together, weaving a thick layer of leaves and branches called the forest canopy. The canopy is so thick that little sunlight gets through to the rain forest floor. Between the canopy and the floor grows a layer of shrubs and small trees that rises about 10 to 50 feet above the floor. This layer is called the understory. Some trees are very tall, and their branches and leaves tower at the top of the canopy. These are emergent trees, and are usually hardwoods, such as mahogany, rosewood, and ebony.

Because the floor of the rain forest is dark and damp, plants that require sunlight do not grow quickly. The few plants that grow there have broad, flat leaves to absorb as much sunlight as possible. Their leaves have waxy surfaces and pointed tips to allow water to run off easily. Other plants along the floor include vines that grow on top of understory shrubs and up tree trunks toward the light in the canopy.

Since the plant life is richer in the canopy than on the floor, so, too, is the animal life. Reptiles, amphibians, birds, and mammals live together in the treetops of the rain forest. These tree-dwelling, or **arboreal**, animals include frogs, snakes, termites, eagles, toucans, parrots, flying squirrels, leopards, bats, and monkeys.

Tundra	Arctic	High Mountain
Rolling plains with no trees; patches of short grass, moss, and small flowering plants	Frozen desert, covered with ice all year long; no plant life	Many different climates, depending on location; can have tropical forests at the bottom; cool forests in the middle; cold tundra higher up; snow

Average Daytime Temperature: 80°F
Average Nighttime Temperature: 70°F
Average Annual Rainfall: 100–200 inches

Tropical Grasslands

Tropical grasslands, often called *savannas*, are biomes located inland at or near the equator.

The seasons in tropical grasslands are called the wet season and the dry season. Because it's hot all year round, the seasons are determined by variations in rainfall, not temperature.

Few plants survive here except for tough grasses and a few hardy types of trees, among them baobabs and acacia, which have thick trunks, deep roots, and waxy, spiny leaves. These features allow them to survive the extreme drought of the dry season.

The thick grasses are food to the millions of savanna animals, among them antelopes, wildebeests, zebras, giraffes, gazelles, rhinos, buffalos, and elephants. Enormous herds of these grazers roam up and down the grasslands following the rains and searching for water and fresh grasses. Other animals, including cheetahs, leopards, and lions, follow the grazers to prey on them. Still others, including hyenas and jackals, scavenge the remains of dead or dying animals. The savannas also support hundred of species of birds, from tiny sunbirds to eagles, and unique reptiles, amphibians, and insects.

Average Daytime Temperature: 80°F
Average Nighttime Temperature: 55°F
Average Annual Rainfall: 10–40 inches

Mediterranean Regions

Mediterranean regions, also called *chaparrals*, are coastal biomes that are cool and moist in the winter and hot and dry in the summer. These biomes support clumps of trees and some widely spread forests.

During hot summer months, drought-resistant evergreens prove the hardiest plants in this scrubland and grass biome. The leaves and stems provide moisture and nutrition for a variety of animals, most of them small enough to seek cover beneath the low branches as they nibble on leaves. Here is a home for rodents—tiny mice and rabbits—and their predators. Underground or deep in shade, lizards wait out the heat of the day. Foxes and hawks, and other predator mammals and birds, stalk and circle to make a meal on the small local fare.

The chaparral is a different place in winter months when it is cooler and wetter. Then plants grow more abundantly and the animal populations surge as well. Even large grazers, such as deer, gather to nibble on the winter foliage.

Average Daytime Temperature:
90°F summer, 55°F winter
Average Nighttime Temperature:
70°F summer, 40°F winter
Average Annual Rainfall: about 10 inches

Temperate Forests

In the areas between the cold polar regions and the hot tropics of both hemispheres are *temperate forests* with warm summers and cool winters.

These temperate forests are dominated by deciduous trees, such as oak, elm, ash, maple, and birch. Evergreens are also present in these forests, including the giant sequoias of the temperate forests in northern California.

In spring and summer, the leaves of the trees provide shade for the forest floor, so temperatures remain cool. Although winters can be cold—often below freezing—the forest remains an inviting environment for many types of plants and animals, from earthworms and insects to songbirds, predator birds, deer, and foxes.

Average Daytime Temperature:
68°F summer, 32°F winter
Average Nighttime Temperature:
58°F summer, 18°F winter
Average Annual Rainfall: about 40 inches

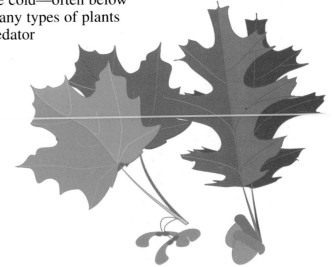

Cool Forests

Also called *boreal* forests, *cool forests* are made up mostly of coniferous (cone-bearing) trees. The conifers grow better than other trees in these cold regions located in the extreme temperate zones and into the polar regions, where summer is short and winter is long and dark. Pine, spruce, and hemlock trees grow here, supplying cover to a few year-round residents, including birds; small mammals such as rodents, rabbits, and squirrels; and large animals such as moose, elk, caribou, and bears.

In the winter, the boreal residents tuck themselves away into natural shelters, many to graze only an hour or two each day in the freezing temperatures, others to hibernate during the months of deepest chill.

But spring brings a full complement of migratory animals, particularly birds, who seek the mild temperatures and abundant food in the cool forest summer. These animals will stay until, as summer turns to autumn, instinct tells them to move back to their tropical winter homes.

Average Daytime Temperature:
65°F summer, 20°F winter
Average Nighttime Temperature:
50°F summer, 10°F winter
Average Annual Rainfall: about 20 inches

Cool Grasslands

Cool grasslands include *prairies* covered in tall grasses and other regions with shorter grasses. These grasslands are drier than cool forest regions, but experience similar summer and winter temperatures.

Few of the cool grassland biomes have been left by human beings in their natural state. That's because the grasslands are excellent for farming both livestock and crops.

Instead of serving as natural grazing lands for large herds of wild animals, the grasslands are now covered in wheat, barley, oats, soybeans, and other grain crops. Populations of cows, sheep, horses, goats, and other domesticated animals feed on the coarse grasses.

Average Daytime Temperature: 75°F summer, 20°F winter
Average Nighttime Temperature: 60°F summer, 0°F winter
Average Annual Rainfall: under 25 inches

Deserts

Deserts are regions—hot or cold—where the land is covered in sand or bare soil and precipitation totals are very small, less than 10 inches each year.

In most hot deserts, temperatures vary greatly, from extremely hot days to cool, even freezing, nights.

Plant and animal life in deserts is well adapted to the harsh environment. Cacti and euphorbia are typical desert plants. Called *succulents*, these plants store water in their waxy leaves and stems. To avoid the hot days, many animals in the desert are *nocturnal*, or active only at night. These animals burrow deep into the earth to spend the daylight hours away from the burning sun. They search for food during the cool nighttime hours. Certain types of lizards and snakes thrive in the hot desert sun, as do animals that need only a little water.

Although we often think of deserts as hot places, not all deserts are hot. The far north of Siberia in Russia and much of Antarctica are cold deserts.

Average Daytime Temperature: 100°F summer, 65°F winter*
Average Nighttime Temperature: 75°F summer, 45°F winter*
Average Annual Rainfall: under 10 inches

*Averages represent hot deserts located in tropical and temperate regions, not frozen deserts.

Tundra

Tundra biomes are extreme climates, too cold for trees to grow. While the top of the ground thaws during the warm season, a layer beneath it, about 10 inches of frozen ground, never melts. It is called *permafrost*.

In this harsh biome, winter is particularly cruel. Yet a few animals remain after the others have migrated south for the winter. Lemmings, ermines, arctic foxes, wolves, musk oxen, reindeer, and polar bears grow heavy winter coats or huddle into dens to keep warm through the long, dark winter.

During the few short months of warm weather, low-growing tundra flowers bloom. Birds and insects newly arrived from the south feast on these, as do herds of moose and caribou that have traveled to the tundra from their winter homes farther south.

Average Daytime Temperature: 55°F summer, 30°F winter
Average Nighttime Temperature: 40°F summer, -10°F winter
Average Annual Rainfall: 30–45 inches

Polar Regions

The *polar regions* are frozen deserts covered in ice all year long. Because it is over land instead of water, the Antarctic is much colder than the Arctic.

The Arctic polar region (around the north pole) is a solid mass of frozen ocean water. The Antarctic polar region (around the south pole) is a mass of frozen land covered in ice and snow. Together, the areas surrounding the north and south poles are known as the *polar ice caps*.

Powerful icy winds blow across the polar ice caps, causing blizzards of snow and ice blown up from the surface. However, little snow actually falls from the skies over the ice caps because the air temperatures are too cold for moisture to evaporate and form clouds.

Only migrating animals, such as polar bears and arctic seals, are found on the Arctic ice mass. Very few animals are hearty enough to survive conditions in Antarctica. The few that do manage it live along the coasts of the continent, relying upon the sea for food and shelter. Among these remarkable animals are such birds as petrels, gulls, terns, albatrosses— and penguins. Penguins are insulated with a thick coat of feathers over skin protected by a thick layer of fat.

In the icy north arctic seas live Arctic mammals. Here dolphins, porpoises, whales, and seals, protected by thick layers of oily fat called *blubber*, swim in the near-freezing waters.

Average Daytime Temperature:	Arctic: 30°F summer, -10°F winter
	Antarctic: 7°F summer, -80°F winter
Average Nighttime Temperature:	Arctic: 10°F summer, -20°F winter
	Antarctic: -50°F summer, -95°F winter
Average Annual Rainfall:	5–20 inches

Mountain Biomes

Because of the changes in altitude (or height above sea level), high mountain environments support a variety of different climates. Depending on the location of the mountain ranges, biomes on high mountains can range from tropical rain forest to tundra and frozen desert. Mountains also help create different biomes. As warm, moist air flows from coastal regions up against mountain ranges on their *windward* sides, the air pushes upward and cools. The cooled water vapor condenses into droplets in the form of clouds. Often these droplets become large enough to fall as rain. Because moisture carrying air is blocked by the mountain ranges, drier climates, such as plains or deserts, often form on the *leeward* sides.

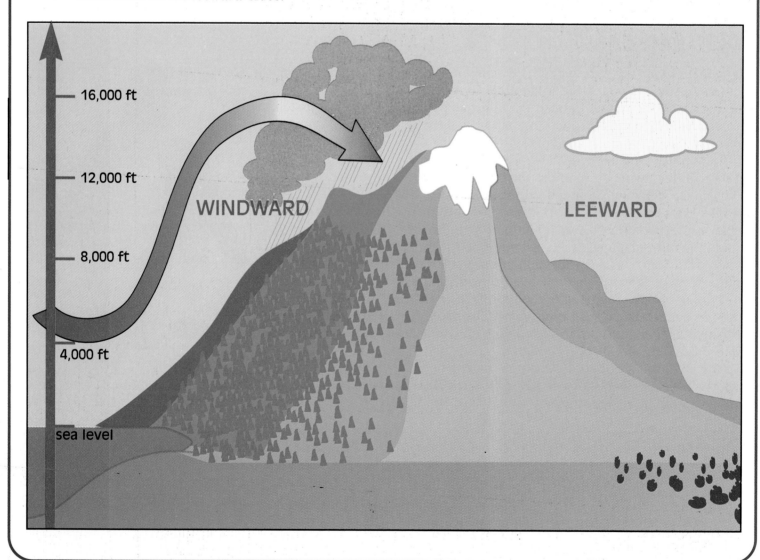

PEOPLE ON LAND AND WATER

Location and Place

What Are Location and Place?

Location is where something—for example, a house, a school, a store, an airport, a mine, or a crop field—is created or built. Location is described in absolute terms (latitude and longitude) or relative terms (north of the road or near the playground). A location becomes a *place* when it is described in terms of its human or physical characteristics.

Climate and landscape, as well as religion, schools, politics, opportunities to make a living, and environmental surroundings give character to a place.

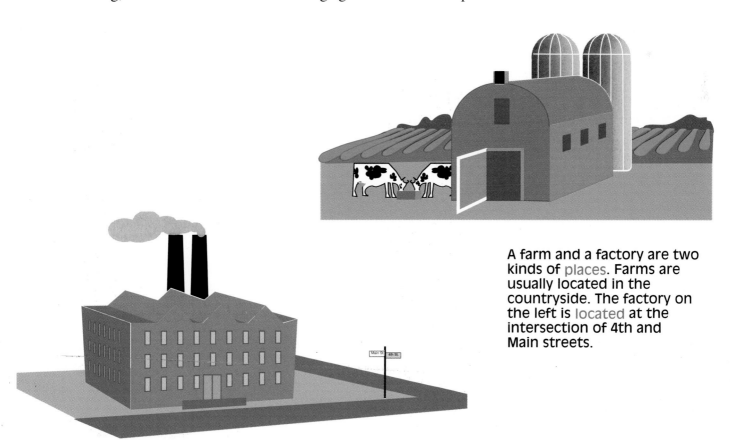

A farm and a factory are two kinds of places. Farms are usually located in the countryside. The factory on the left is located at the intersection of 4th and Main streets.

2 Counting People: Population

Population

Population is the total number of people who live in a particular place. Geographers study population to understand where people live and why they live there.

World Population Growth

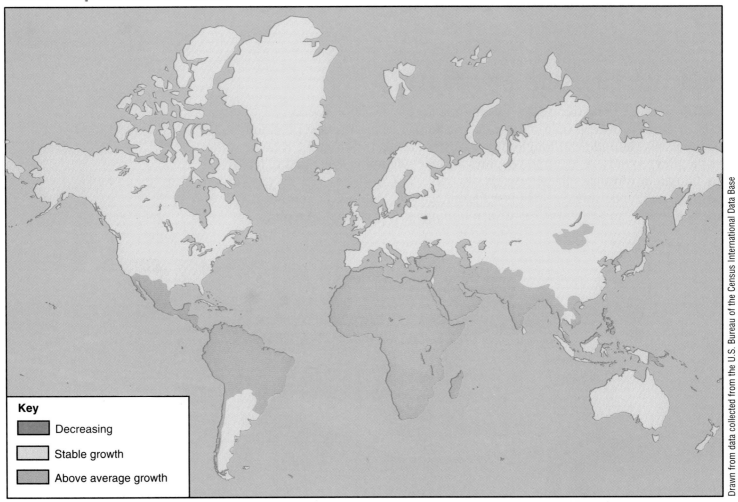

Key
- Decreasing
- Stable growth
- Above average growth

Drawn from data collected from the U.S. Bureau of the Census International Data Base

A map of world population growth shows areas where the number of people is growing, decreasing, or remaining about the same.

 The study of population is called demographics. *The scientists who study demographics are called* demographers.

World Population Growth, 1600–Present

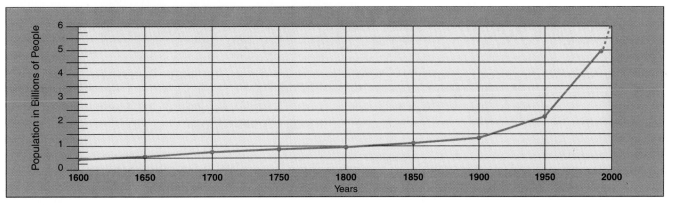

This graph shows world population in billions of people over the last 400 years.

Population Data

In studying human populations, geographers use a lot of different information called **population data**. These data include basic facts about human populations—past, present, and projected into the future.

Some Types of Population Data

1 **Average family size** — The average number of children in a family in a particular culture group or region

2 **Birthrate** — The number of babies born per year per thousand people

3 **Death rate** — The number of people who die per year per thousand people

4 **Doubling time** — The time needed for a population to increase 100 percent, or to double

5 **Life expectancy** — The average number of years people live

6 **Population growth rate** — How quickly a population grows each year measured in percent

7 **Population structure** — The makeup of a population by age and gender (male or female)

The world's population increases by about three people every second. That's nearly 200 people a minute, 10,000 people an hour, and 240,000 people a day!

Population Pictures

Profiles and Pyramids

Geographers use graphs to compare populations in different areas. Two of the most common graphs are the *population profile* and the *population pyramid*.

Population Profile

A *population profile* is a bar graph that shows the different age groups of a population that shares something in common, such as language, dog ownership, or a school.

Population Pyramid

A *population pyramid* is a bar graph that depicts a total population by breaking it down into age groupings and gender.

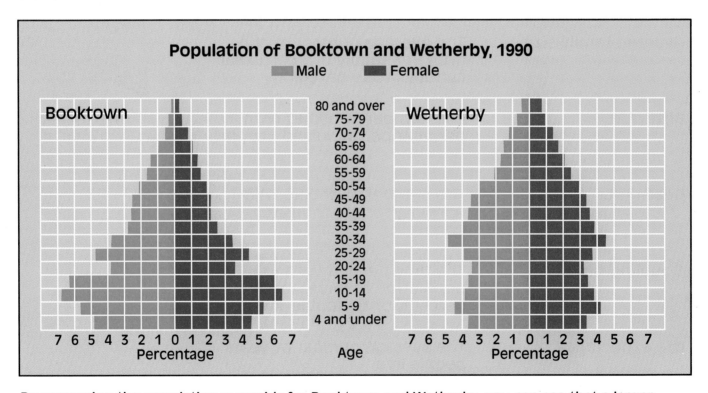

Population of Booktown and Wetherby, 1990

Male   Female

By comparing the population pyramids for Booktown and Wetherby, you can see that a larger percentage of Booktown's population is aged 10–19 than Wetherby's. That is because the Boys Academy of Reading, an all-male middle and high school, brings hundreds of school-age boys into Booktown each year, skewing the population in that age group.

Population Density and Distribution

Population density means how close together people live in a particular place. To find population density, divide the number of people in a place by the total area of that place.

Population distribution or *patterns* tell geographers where most people live within a place or region.

Maps show both population density and distribution. This map shows the population density and distribution in the state of Wisconsin. More than half of the 5,000,000 residents live in cities located in the southeastern and south central parts of the state. Located in these areas are the largest cities in the state: Milwaukee, Madison, and Green Bay.

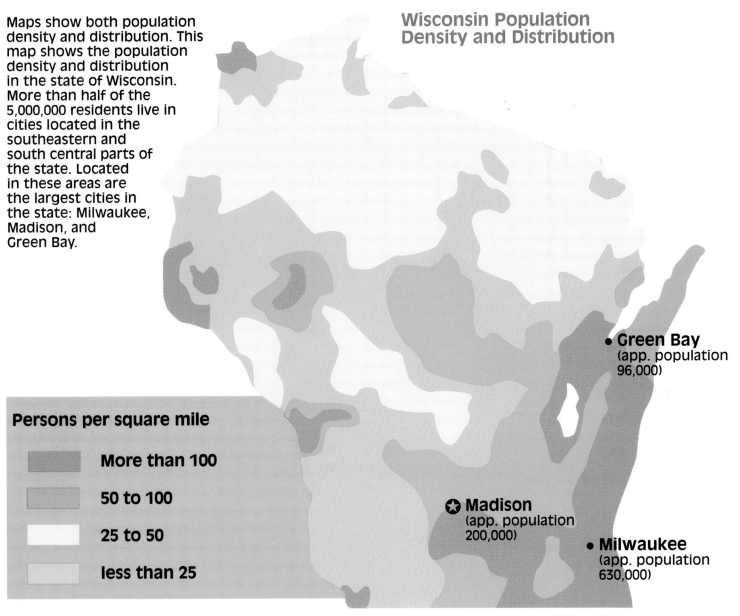

Wisconsin Population Density and Distribution

● **Green Bay** (app. population 96,000)

✪ **Madison** (app. population 200,000)

● **Milwaukee** (app. population 630,000)

Persons per square mile

More than 100

50 to 100

25 to 50

less than 25

Drawn from data gathered by the U.S. Bureau of the Census

Urban vs. Rural

About half the earth's people live in cities and towns, called **urban areas**.
The other half live on farms or in countryside villages, called **rural areas**.

Population patterns: Urban vs. Rural

Key

Isolated settlements

Most population in countryside

Most population in cities

Drawn from data collected from the U.S. Bureau of the Census International Data Base

A map of population patterns shows where people live mostly in cities (urban) and where people live mostly in the countryside (rural).

A Model City, A Model Countryside

A *city*, or *metropolis*, is a large or important town. Sometimes a city grows so large that it grows into a neighboring city, forming a *megalopolis*. But no matter how big it is, a city is made up of a variety of areas.

Businesses and industries are located in the *commercial areas* of a city. Stores and service businesses often are located in *downtown* commercial areas, or the main business area of a city, called the central business district (CBD). Manufacturing and heavy industry (see p. 75) are usually located along the outer edges of a city on major transportation routes (roads, waterways, trains, airports, etc.).

People's homes are located in the *residential* areas of a city. Homes are also found in the *suburbs*, or the residential districts lying just outside a city or town. Like the people who live in the residential areas of a city, people who live in the suburbs usually work in the city and benefit from the services the city offers. Beyond the suburbs are *exurbs*, sparsely populated residential areas.

Most cities are divided into *neighborhoods*, each with its own special cultural makeup. Some neighborhoods are made up of people with the same ethnic or religious backgrounds. For example, many U.S. cities have Chinese, Italian, Korean, or African-American neighborhoods. Other neighborhoods are unique because of their architecture or the era in which they were built. Many U.S. cities have preserved their "historical districts" or the "old cities" where the oldest buildings in the city stand. Still other neighborhoods are defined by physical features. Terms such as "riverside," "highlands," and "flats" are often used to describe neighborhoods within cities.

Outside cities are small towns, villages, and other rural communities, as well as farmland, forests, parks, and other tracts of land. Highways, smaller roads, waterways, railroads, and other transportation routes connect rural areas to each other and to nearby cities, states, or even foreign countries.

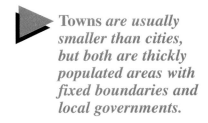

Towns *are usually smaller than cities, but both are thickly populated areas with fixed boundaries and local governments.*

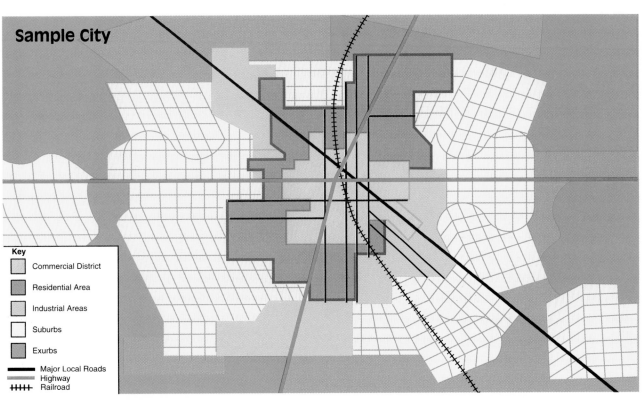

Sample City

Key
- ▨ Commercial District
- ▨ Residential Area
- ▨ Industrial Areas
- ☐ Suburbs
- ▨ Exurbs
- ▬▬ Major Local Roads
- ▬▬ Highway
- ╫╫╫ Railroad

Like most cities, Sample City is made up of several distinct areas, including a downtown, industrial district, residential neighborhoods, and suburbs.

World Birthrates: 1910–1990

Rate of Births
(per 1,000 people per year)

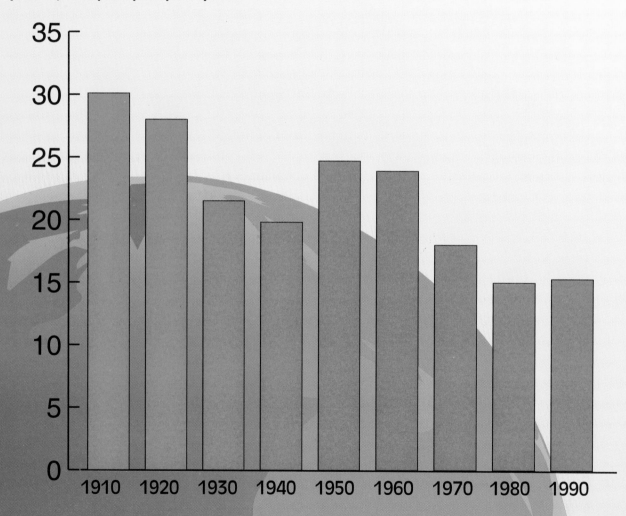

3 Culture

What Is Culture?

Culture is a word used to describe how groups of people act: how we live, what we eat, what we believe, and how we change our environment to create communities.

Geographers who study culture try to explain how people behaved in the past compared with how we behave today. They compare the way people in different areas live their lives. They study languages, beliefs and traditions, political systems, and the technologies that bind communities together or make them different from other communities.

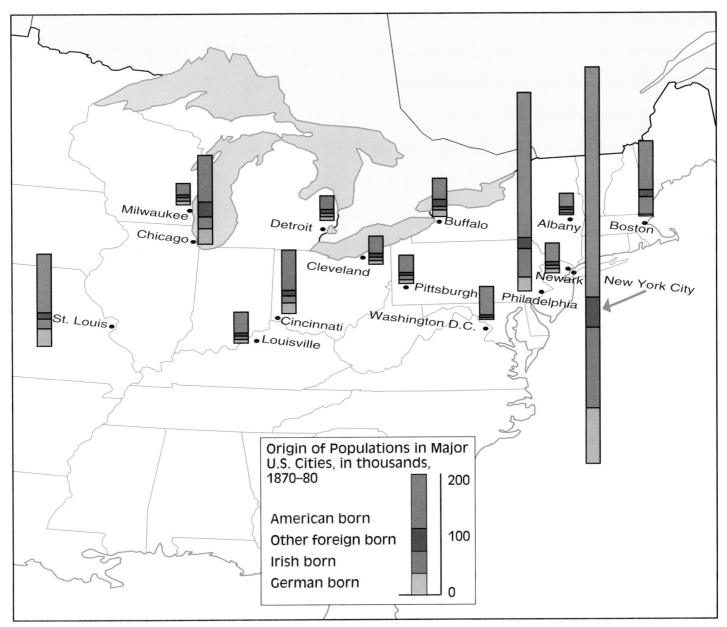

Origin of Populations in Major U.S. Cities, in thousands, 1870–80

- American born
- Other foreign born
- Irish born
- German born

200
100
0

This cultural map compares the Irish and German populations to other foreign-born and American-born citizens of major northern and midwestern American cities over 100 years ago.

The Cultural Mosaic

Geographers consider each culture group to consist of different pieces, like the pieces in a *mosaic*, a picture made by fitting together separate tiles, stones, or glass pieces. Viewed together, the pieces that make up a culture create a picture of that culture, called a *cultural mosaic*.

Elements of the cultural mosaic can be witnessed in a typical American suburban backyard. The types of clothes we wear, the food we eat, the games we play, and the architecture of our homes are all pieces of our cultural mosaic.

Culture Basics

Language

Language is the use of voice sounds, gestures, and written symbols
to communicate thoughts and feelings.

Language Families

More than 2,800 languages are spoken in the world today. These languages
have been grouped into several *language families*. Here are some of the
main groups.

*The five languages
most spoken in the
world today are
Mandarin Chinese,
English, Hindi,
Russian, and Spanish.*

FAMILY	APPROXIMATE NUMBER OF SPEAKERS	PRINCIPAL LANGUAGES
Indo-European	2.6 billion	Latvian, Lithuanian, Belorussian, Bulgarian, Czech, Macedonian, Polish, Russian, Serb, Croatian, Slovak, Slovenian, Ukranian, Irish, Scots Gaelic, Dutch, English, German, Norwegian, Danish, Swedish, Icelandic, Bengali, Gujarati, Hindi, Marathi, Punjabi, Urdu, Iranian, French, Italian, Portuguese, Romanian, Spanish
Sino-Tibetan	1.2 billion	Chinese, Thai, Burmese, Tibetan
Black African	440 million	Includes Niger-Kordofanian, Nilo-Saharan, and Khoisan Language families
Malayo-Polynesian	275 million	Indonesian, Tagalog, Maori
Afro-Asian	220 million	Arabic, Hebrew, Berber, Amharic
Dravidian	220 million	Tamil, Telugu
Japanese and Korean	200 million	Japanese and Korean
Uralic-Altaic	165 million	Finnish, Estonian, Hungarian, Turkish
Mon-Khmer	110 million	Khmer and Laotian

*Slang is language used instead of standard vocabulary. It is usually used to provide emphasis or humor in speech and, sometimes, in writing. A **dialect** is a variation of a standard language spoken by a particular group of people. A dialect differs from standard language in grammar, vocabulary, or pronunciation, or in any combination of the three.*

Language Barriers

Throughout early history, mountains have stopped the spread of language. So have large bodies of water, deserts, and thick jungles. Because people couldn't cross these barriers easily, groups of people on opposite sides developed languages separately. So, people on one side of a geographic barrier might speak a language different from people on the other. Today these boundaries are no longer difficult to cross, yet they help explain the diversity of world languages.

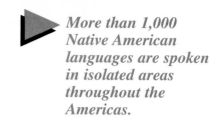

More than 1,000 Native American languages are spoken in isolated areas throughout the Americas.

World Language Families

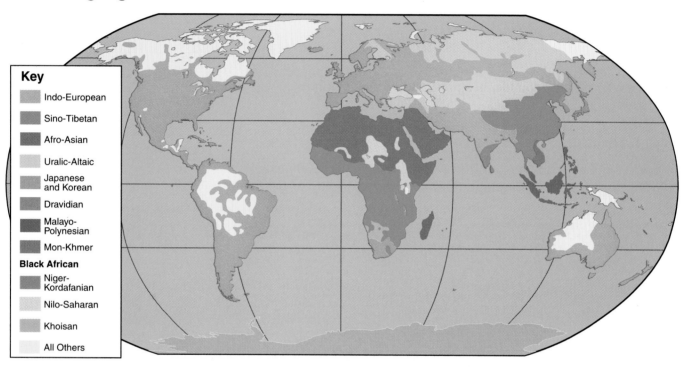

Key
- Indo-European
- Sino-Tibetan
- Afro-Asian
- Uralic-Altaic
- Japanese and Korean
- Dravidian
- Malayo-Polynesian
- Mon-Khmer

Black African
- Niger-Kordafanian
- Nilo-Saharan
- Khoisan
- All Others

Beliefs and Traditions: Religions, Customs, and Arts and Crafts

Beliefs are the attitudes, ideas, and world views held by a person or a group of people. Every culture has a set of beliefs, or a **belief system**. This system is made up of three basic elements:

1	Religion	A belief in and legends about a god or gods who created the world and affect peoples' lives
2	Customs and manners	The traditions people have or ways people act or behave in a group
3	Arts and crafts	The clothing, music, arts, architecture, tools, etc., used by a group

Religion

Over the centuries, people have believed in many religions. Today, dozens of religions are practiced in the world. However, five major religions are the most widely practiced.

Major World Religions

1 Hinduism Begun about 1500 B.C. in India. Hindus believe in many gods and in reincarnation (rebirth of the soul after death). Today, Hinduism is practiced by 764,000,000 people primarily in India, Nepal, Malaysia, Guyana, Suriname, and Sri Lanka.

2 Judaism Begun about 1300 B.C. among the Hebrew people in the Middle East. Judaism was the first religion founded on a belief in one god rather than a group of gods. Today, Judaism is practiced by 13,500,000 people throughout the world, primarily in Israel, Europe, and the United States.

3 Buddhism Begun about 525 B.C. by Siddhartha Gautama (Buddha), c. 563–480, in India. Buddhists follow the Hindu belief in reincarnation, and they work to gain inner peace, called Nirvana. Today, Buddhism is practiced by approximately 338,500,000 people throughout Asia, from Sri Lanka to Japan.

4 Christianity Begun in the first century in the Middle East among Jews who believed that Jesus of Nazareth was the divine son of god. Today, Christianity is practiced by approximately 1,900,000,000 people throughout the world, primarily in Europe, North America, South America, and Africa, as well as in pockets of Asia.

5 Islam Begun in A.D. 622 in the Middle East by followers of Muhammad. Islam includes many of the features of Judaism and Christianity, including the belief in one god, which Moslems call Allah. Today, Islam is practiced by 1,033,450,000 people, primarily in the western and northern countries of Africa, throughout the Middle East, Central Asia, western China, Malaysia, Indonesia, the Philippines, and the United States.

The rest of the world's population, approximately 1,600,000,000 people, practices other religions or no religion.

Customs and Manners

Customs are the usual habits of a group of people. *Manners*, or norms, are the habits considered to be polite among a group of people. Both customs and manners are the result of what a group considers important: its values. For example, when a young person offers a seat to an older person, the custom demonstrates the value of respect for one's elders.

GREETINGS!
Manners, Meanings, and Cultural Differences

What is accepted as polite behavior in one place isn't necessarily so in another.

Waving with the palm of the hand facing out is a gesture of greeting in America and most European cultures. In Turkey and Greece, however, the gesture is called "The Hand of Moutza," and is considered a serious insult.

In the United States, people often shake hands as a greeting or when they are introduced to new people. In Japan and India, touch is not used in greetings. In Japan, people bow to acknowledge new contacts or to express respect to old friends. In India, people touch their palms together, prayer-style, to show welcome.

Sticking out the tongue is considered rude in the United States, but among the Aborigines in Australia, it is a sign of greeting and affection. In China, it is a sign of embarrassment.

Arts and Crafts

Art communicates the values and beliefs of a culture in what that culture finds beautiful. It can include paintings, sculpture, plays, poems, dance, photographs, movies, novels, and music.

Crafts refers to useful items and the methods used to make them. Crafts include sewing, weaving, tools for cooking, farming, mining, manufacturing, and the design and construction of buildings (architecture).

 All the art forms—visual arts, music, literature, and dance—together are called the fine arts.

Culture Crafts

Hand-woven baskets, woolen blankets and rugs, pottery, and ivory needles—among many other items—have been used for centuries in different cultures throughout the world. Created for everyday use, many of these items are now considered art objects. That means their value is measured both in their usefulness and their beauty.

Home, Sweet Home
The Architecture of Houses

Plantation-style houses have been built around the world by European settlers. This particular style of house, however, is most often seen in agricultural or tropical regions.

People in different culture groups tend to build different kinds of houses. The differences include:

1. Building materials: Some cultures build homes of wood, some of stone, some of earth. People build homes with the materials available in their geographical regions.

2. Beauty: People build homes that look pleasing to them, homes that fit their idea of beauty. In Europe, even new homes are built to look like those that have stood in villages for hundreds of years. Among the Bedouin of North Africa, homes are not permanent structures, but brilliantly colored tents festooned with tassels and fringes.

3. Use: People build homes primarily for shelter but also to fit the way they live. A Masai cattle herder needs a place within his home, or **shamba**, to corral livestock. An Inuit needs shelter from the Arctic winds yet access to fishing. An American suburbanite needs to be near transportation to the city. Homes are also designed to suit different climates and amounts of space. For example, many houses in cold climates are insulated between the inside and outside walls, floors, and ceilings. In tropical climates, walls made of a single layer of bamboo or reeds provide shelter from the hot sun.

Teepees were once homes to some of the members of the Plains Nations of Native Americans.

Houses built along the rivers and rice paddies of Asia are often built on stilts to protect dwellers from rising and falling water levels.

Food! Glorious Food!

What people in a group eat is part of their culture. The food culture is created by tastes and influenced by religion and customs. A group's diet is also determined by what it can grow or raise. Climate, too, influences how people build their kitchens and prepare their foods. Location determines dietary factors in many cultures. However, nowadays, because of excellent transportation and storage, canned goods are found in the homes of Arctic Inuits and frozen meals in the homes of people in desert regions.

Cuisine *means a particular style of cooking or preparing food. Cuisine is determined by everything from taste to climate, farming, and location. For example, the cuisines of Asia use rice as a main ingredient. In Italian cuisine, wheat flour noodles called pasta are common. Cuisine is another way of saying "food culture." Today, with mass communication, migration, and transportation, many cuisines are available all over the world. Chinese and Italian cuisines, for example, are enjoyed by people in restaurants all over North America. Once an American phenomenon, fast foods, such as hamburgers and fries, are available in cities as far apart as Beijing, China, and São Paulo, Brazil.*

Political Systems

Political systems are governments, or the ruling bodies of the world's peoples.
People who live under one government form a *country* or *nation*.

What Is Government?

Political systems or *governments* provide a set of laws and rules. There are many types of political systems, including:

Anarchy	**No government or organized authority.**
Confederacy	**An alliance of separately governed states.**
Democracy	**A nation in which power rests with the people and is exercised directly by them or their elected representatives.**
Dictatorship	**A nation in which absolute power is controlled by a person whose position is not inherited.**
Empire	**A group of nations or territories ruled by one leader or country.**
Monarchy	**A nation ruled by a supreme sovereign, such as a king, queen, or emperor. In most monarchies, the rulers inherit their power. A constitutional monarchy is a system in which a king or queen is the head of state in a country ruled by a separate government.**
Parliamentary Government	**An assembly of persons, not necessarily elected, who make up the laws of a nation or state.**
Republic	**A nation without a monarch and, in modern times, usually led by a president.**

How People Live

The Hunter-Gatherers

In ancient societies, people lived as *hunter-gatherers.* In some places today, they still do. That means they hunt, fish, and forage from the wild to find food.

Subsistence Farmers

To feed themselves, humans learned to sow plants and grow crops as well as to hunt and gather food. Over time, farmers learned to raise enough food to feed themselves.

Farmers who raise just enough food to feed themselves and their families are called *subsistence farmers*. Subsistence farming is still common in several parts of the world. In other parts, farming has become an industry or commercial activity (see below).

INDUSTRY & TECHNOLOGY

Industry means making products not simply for your use or your family's, but for sale to other people. Industries are divided into two categories: light and heavy.

Light industries   use lightweight raw materials to make clothes, food products, plants and flowers, furniture, and other consumer goods.

Heavy industries   produce machines that do big jobs, such as cranes, oil derricks, cars, ships, airplanes, and farm equipment.

There are many different types of light and heavy industries, but most fall into one of five categories:

1. Agriculture

2. Mining

3. Forestry

4. Fishing and fishery

5. Manufacturing

Technology is the use of scientific knowledge, usually to improve industry and commerce. Technology includes the machines and other tools used to work in a variety of industries, manufacturing (see p. 81), and arts and crafts (see p. 71).

Agriculture

Agriculture means farming. Farming began more than 10,000 years ago. Unlike hunter-gatherers who roamed from one place to another to find food, farmers built permanent homes and farmed the same land in the same area year after year.

Most of the food we eat and many of the materials for the things we use are grown on farms.

Some farms only grow plants, or crops, for food (fresh vegetables and fruits) or manufacture (wheat for flour, soybeans for meat substitutes, cotton for fabrics, corn for feed, etc.). Other farms use the land to graze animals. These are called livestock farms, and include farms where animals are grown to be processed into meats or where they are grown to provide milk for dairy products (milk, cream, butter, cheese) and eggs. Some farms produce both crops and livestock. (These are called mixed farms.)

Old MacDonald Had a Farm

Old MacDonald had a farm—but just what kind of farm was it?

cooperative farm	Farm owned and operated by a group of farmers for the benefit of each individual involved.
corporate farm	Farm owned by a corporation, usually producing goods for sale in stores under a company label.
crop farm	Farm that raises crops for harvest, such as vegetables, fruits, or grains.
dairy farm	Farm specializing in the production of milk, cheese, butter, and other dairy products.
family farm	Farm owned and operated by a family as a private business.
livestock farm	Farm specializing in growing animals, such as chickens, pigs, cows, goats, or buffalo, for egg, dairy, or meat production.
mixed farm	Farm where both livestock and crops are grown.
ranch	Farm specializing in one type of crop or livestock, such as a cattle ranch, mink ranch, or deer ranch.
subsistence farm	Farm on which food and other products necessary for life are grown by one family for its own use.
commercial farm	Farm specializing in products for sale to a wide market and intended to make profits from sales instead of products for family use.
plantation	Large farm or estate in tropical or semitropical areas, often specializing in commercial crops, such as cotton, tobacco, rice, sugar cane, coffee, or tea.
truck farm	Farm close to a city that specializes in vegetables, fruit, and other cash crops.
herding farm	Farm that uses large areas of land, usually arid, for herding goats, camels, sheep, and/or cattle.

World Agriculture

World Agricultural Work Force

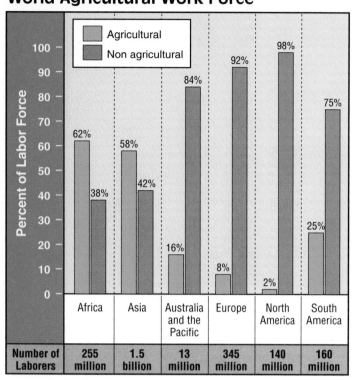

| Number of Laborers | 255 million | 1.5 billion | 13 million | 345 million | 140 million | 160 million |

World Crop Production by Continent

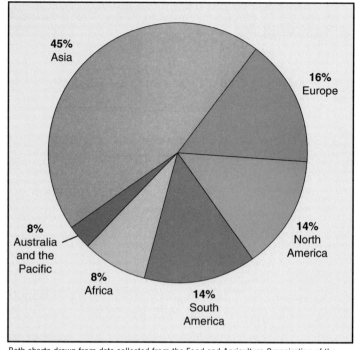

Both charts drawn from data collected from the Food and Agriculture Organization of the United Nations (1992)

More than half the labor force—or more than 1 billion people—in Asia and Africa work in agriculture, whereas only approximately 12%—or about 75 million people—work in agriculture in the rest of the world. Yet these 75 million people produce almost half the world's crops. By comparing these graphs, you might conclude that most of the farming in Asia and Africa is subsistence farming, not commercial farming.

Mining

Mining means taking rocks and minerals out of the earth. Many different rocks and minerals are mined, although they all fall into one of four categories:

Category	Example
metals	iron, lead, gold, silver, platinum
gemstones	diamonds, emeralds, rubies, sapphires, amethyst, lapis lazuli, jade
fossil fuels	natural gas, oil, coal
conglomerates	rock, sand, gravel

 Some rocks and minerals are harder than others. The hardness is measured on the Mohs scale, a scale devised by the German scientist Friedrich Mohs. It ranks all rocks from 1 to 10.

MOHS SCALE

Softest	1	Talc
	2	Gypsum
	3	Calcite
	4	Fluorite
	5	Apatite
	6	Feldspar
	7	Quartz
	8	Topaz
	9	Corundum
Hardest	10	Diamond

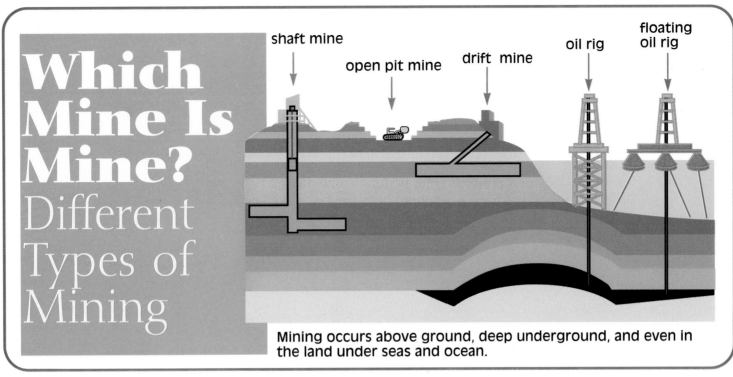

Which Mine Is Mine?
Different Types of Mining

shaft mine

open pit mine

drift mine

oil rig

floating oil rig

Mining occurs above ground, deep underground, and even in the land under seas and ocean.

 Some mineral resources are running low. If we continue to use minerals at our current rate, silver, gold, copper, natural gas, oil, iron ore, and uranium could be in short supply by 2050. However, because we recognize the danger, some people are using minerals more carefully. Also, geologists are searching for new deposits of these precious minerals, on land and in the oceans.

Forestry

Forestry is the growing, maintaining, and harvesting of forests. Forests provide us with wood, which is used for building materials, furniture, paper, fuel, gums and resins, waxes, and medicines.

The world's forests come in many sizes and are filled with many different types of trees.

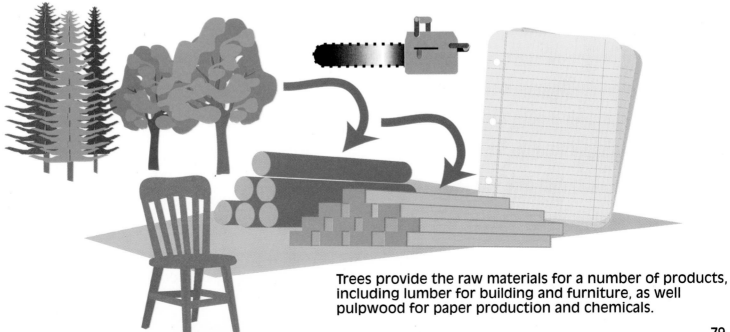

Trees provide the raw materials for a number of products, including lumber for building and furniture, as well pulpwood for paper production and chemicals.

Fishing and Fisheries

The business of fishing is called *fishery*, and includes not only the catching and farming of fish and other aquatic animals, but also their processing and selling. Fishing is big business around the world. Nearly 80 million tons of sea animals are caught each year.

Manufacturing

Manufacturing means making new products from both raw materials and recycled materials. *Raw materials* are the natural products used to make new products. *Recycled materials* are the glass, metal, plastic, and paper collected from trash that are processed and reused to make new products.

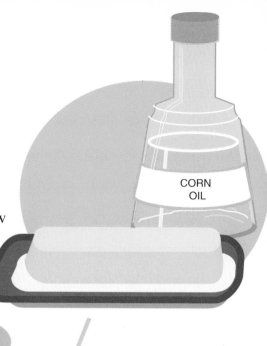

CORN OIL

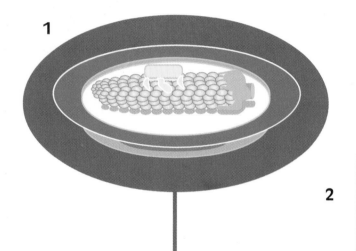

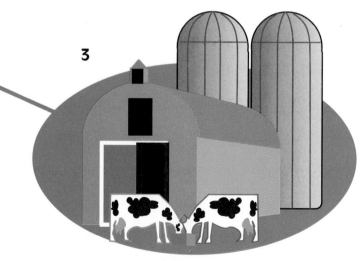

Corn is a versatile raw material. It is used as: 1. a food crop; 2. a raw material for producing corn oil and other processed foods and materials; and 3. a feed crop to support livestock.

A Brief History of Manufacturing

Machines such as the spinning wheel made cottage industries possible.

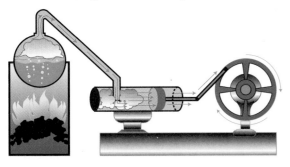

James Watt patented his steam engine in 1769, and the Industrial Revolution began.

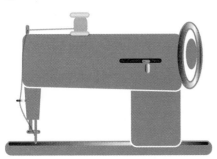

The sewing machine made the creation of clothes easier for homemakers. It also made possible the garment industry because clothes could be mass-produced with the aid of this time-saving machine.

Before the 1700s, most people manufactured goods for their own use in their homes. People wove fleece and plant fibers into fabrics and made their own clothes. They caught fish and raised crops, and preserved and canned them. They cut trees to burn as fuel and to use as lumber to build houses, barns, fences, and more.

Later, people made things for other people from within their homes. For example, a tailor would sew not only for himself or herself, but also for those who paid for the service. A farmer might grow extra crops to sell at a farm stand, or a lumberer might fell logs for other people to build with or burn as firewood. People still manufacture products in their homes or in small local factories. These home-based manufacturing operations are called *cottage industries*.

In Europe, the early 1700s brought machines that made work easier and the production of manufactured products quicker and cheaper. The most important of these machines was improved and patented by the British inventor James Watt in 1769. It was the steam engine, and it brought about a change in the way people in Europe and the New World made products. This period of change is called the *Industrial Revolution*.

With the Industrial Revolution came many changes in the world of manufacturing and business. For example, instead of making one product at a time, the machines of the Industrial Revolution allowed for *mass production*, or the creation of many of the same product at the same time.

Many factory owners earned a great deal of money by selling mass-produced products. They built huge factories to make more and more products. To operate these factories, they hired many people. In fact, huge numbers of people moved into cities and factory towns during the Industrial Revolution to find work, live, and raise families.

Then, as today, businesses built or bought up other factories in different towns, cities, or even different states or countries. Companies with factories in two or more countries are called *multinational companies*.

Many items are produced on assembly lines, where different workers are responsible for separate tasks in the creation of a product. Cars are mass-produced, usually on assembly lines.

ALASKA
(U.S.)

Beaufort Sea

Gulf of Alaska

CANADA

Hudson Bay

GREENLAND
(KALAALLIT NUNAAT)
(DENMARK)

Baffin Bay

Greenland Sea

Arctic Circle

NORWA

ICELAND   DENMARK

THE NETHERLANDS

BELGIUM

UNITED
KINGDOM

IRELAND

ATLANTIC
OCEAN

UNITED STATES OF AMERICA

MEXICO

Gulf of Mexico

CUBA

BAHAMAS

HAITI

JAMAICA

Tropic of Cancer

HAWAIIAN
ISLANDS
(U.S.)

PACIFIC
OCEAN

BELIZE
GUATEMALA
EL SALVADOR
HONDURAS
NICARAGUA
COSTA RICA
PANAMA

Caribbean Sea

DOMINICAN
REPUBLIC
PUERTO RICO (U.S.)
VIRGIN ISLANDS (U.S., U.K.)
ST. KITTS AND NEVIS
ANTIGUA AND BARBUDA
DOMINICA
ST. LUCIA
ST. VINCENT
AND THE GRENADINES
BARBADOS
GRENADA
TRINIDAD AND TOBAGO

VENEZUELA

GUYANA
SURINAME
FRENCH
GUIANA
(FRANCE)

COLOMBIA

ECUADOR

Equator

PERU

BRAZIL

BOLIVIA

PARAGUAY

OLUXEMBOURG
SWITZERLAND
OLIECHTENSTEIN
SLOVENIA
CROATIA
OMONACO
OANDORRA
BOSNIA AND HERZEGOVINA
PORTUGAL
SPAIN

FRANCE

SAN
MARINO
OVATICAN CI
SERBIA AND
MONTENEGRO
ALBANIA
MACEDONIA
TU

CANARY
ISLANDS
(SPAIN)

MOROCCO

WESTERN
SAHARA
(disputed)

OCAPE VERDE

MAURITANIA

ALGERIA

MALI

N

SENEGAL
OGAMBIA
GUINEA-BISSAU
GUINEA
SIERRA LEONE
LIBERIA

BURKINA
FASO

NIGE

CÔTE D'IVOIRE
GHANA
TOGO
BENIN

OSÃO TOM
AND PRINCIPE

CAMF

GABO

OEQUATORIAL
GUINEA

CONG

ANGOL

TAHITI
(FRANCE)

Tropic of Capricorn

30°S

CHILE

URUGUAY

ARGENTINA

FALKLAND ISLANDS
(ISLAS MALVINAS)
(U.K.)

Cape Horn

60°S

Antarctic Circle

ANTARCTI

Cap
Good

NAM

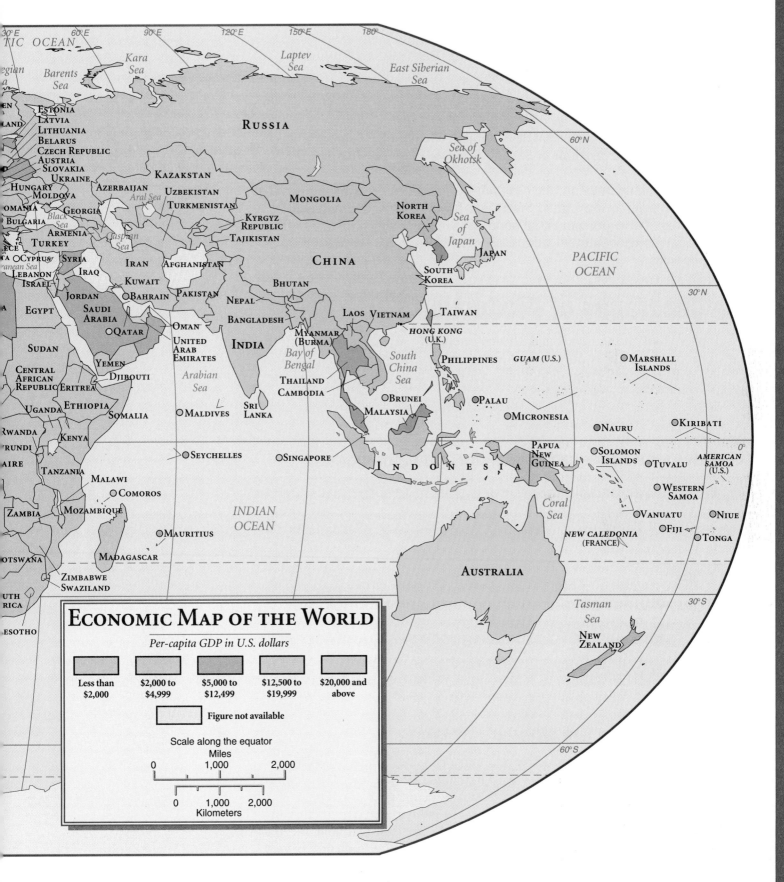

ECONOMIC MAP OF THE WORLD

Per-capita GDP in U.S. dollars

Less than $2,000	$2,000 to $4,999	$5,000 to $12,499	$12,500 to $19,999	$20,000 and above

Figure not available

Scale along the equator

Miles
0   1,000   2,000

Kilometers
0   1,000   2,000

Measuring Economies

Geographers study and compare the economies of different places. One way they measure an economy is by how much industry, sometimes called industrial development, a place has. Some countries, such as Taiwan and Russia, have lots of factories to turn natural resources into manufactured goods. They are considered *industrially developed*.

Other places, such as Mexico, are considered *developing countries* because they have some industry but need more. Still others, such as those of Chad or Cambodia, have little industrial development. Geographers consider the natural resources underused, or underdeveloped, in these *pre-industrial economies*.

Geographers sometimes use the term *postindustrial* to describe industrialized countries, such as the United States and Japan, no longer dominated by heavy industry. These postindustrial countries employ many workers to gather information, manage communications, and perform various services, such as banking or sales.

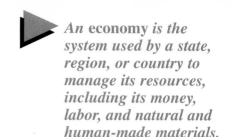

An economy is the system used by a state, region, or country to manage its resources, including its money, labor, and natural and human-made materials.

The Geography of Production

Geographers look at the goods and services a country produces, including the tons of crops, the number of cars, and the number of people working in different jobs. Added together, the output of a country is called its *gross domestic product* (GDP). (See also pp. 82–83.)

High GDPs

Countries with advanced machinery and technology:

> 1. Need fewer people to produce goods and supply services.

> 2. Create goods and provide services quickly and efficiently.

Low GDPs

Countries without advanced machinery and technology:

> 1. Need more people to produce goods and supply services.

> 2. Create fewer goods and provide services more slowly and less efficiently.

Development and the Standard of Living

While GDP measures how productive a country is, geographers use another measurement when they look at how well individual people live. The *standard of living* shows how well the average person is able to find a job, a place to live, food, and an education. Generally, the more industrialized a country, the higher its standard of living. But this is not always true. For example, the standard of living in Kuwait, which has lots of oil but little other industry, is very high. On the other hand, one reason people in the former Soviet Union were dissatisfied is that they had a very low standard of living although their nation had a lot of industry.

Migration, from Exploration to Settlement

An Overview of Migration

Scientists who study migration hypothesize that the first humans were born in Africa more than two million years ago and spread out from there into other parts of the world.

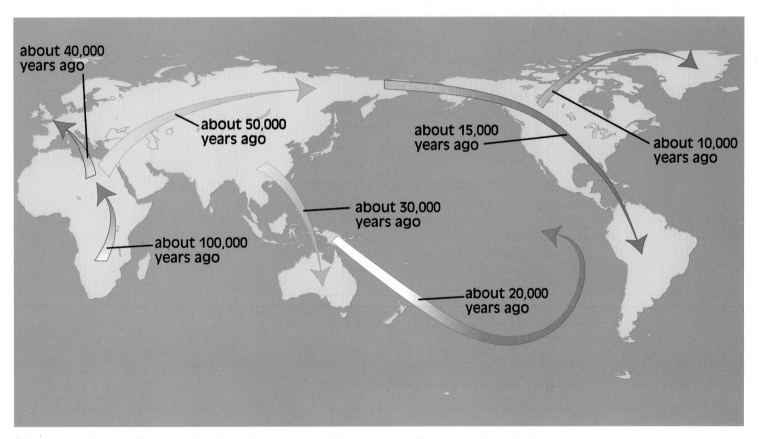

about 40,000 years ago

about 50,000 years ago

about 15,000 years ago

about 10,000 years ago

about 30,000 years ago

about 100,000 years ago

about 20,000 years ago

Many scientists and geographers believe that humans moved from Africa into Europe and Asia between 40 and 50 thousand years ago, then, over the next 30,000 years, spread further to inhabit all the continents, except Antarctica, and many Pacific islands.

CONQUEST AND EMPIRE

In Europe in the late 1400s, an era called the Age of Exploration began. During this era, explorers made voyages to areas unknown to Europeans. Soon Europeans began to colonize and settle in many new places.

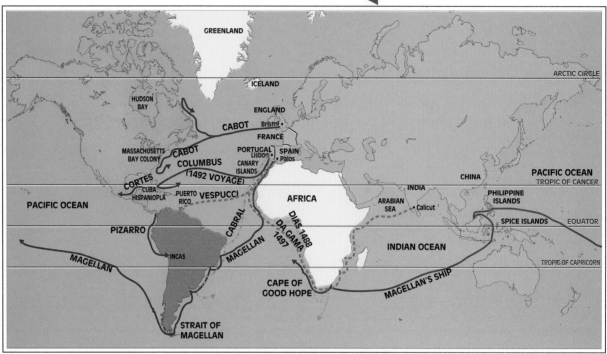

Routes of some major voyages led by European explorers.

Migration *means movement from one place to settle in another.*
Emigration *means movement* **away** *from one's homeland.*
Immigration *means movement* **into** *a new country.*

Can't Get There from Here: TRANSPORTATION

In order for people to move from one region to another, they need *transportation* for themselves and their possessions. Early transportation was by foot. People simply walked from one place to another. Later, animals—horses, mules, and oxen—were tamed and used to carry passengers or packages, as well as to pull carts, sleds, and carriages.

With the Industrial Revolution (see p. 81) came the invention of machines to transport people farther in less time.

One of the products of the Industrial Revolution was the automobile.

Why Move?

People usually move from one place to another in search of a better place to live. Although there are many things that make one place better or worse than another, these things fall into two main categories:

1. Economics

2. Politics

People move away from:	To:	
Poverty	Areas of greater wealth	Economic Reasons
Overcrowded conditions	Greater space and comfort	
High cost of living	Affordable goods, services, and housing	
Lack of jobs	More work opportunities	Economic and Political Reasons
Poor schools	Greater educational opportunities	
Poor health care	Available, higher quality, health care	Political Reasons
Intolerance of race, culture, or religion.	Tolerance	
Political oppression	Political choice and rights	
War or crime	Peaceful, safe life	

APPENDIX

1. Glossary of Geographical Terms

acid rain Rain that is polluted by acid in the atmosphere and damages the environment.

agriculture Using the land to grow crops and raise animals; farming (see p. 77).

Antarctic Circle A line of latitude that lies 66 degrees 30 minutes (66° 30´) south of the equator. From September 21 to December 21, the area north of the Antarctic Circle has daylight more than 12 hours a day. On December 21 it is daylight for 24 hours at the Antarctic Circle. Then the days get shorter until there is darkness for 24 hours on June 21.

aquifer A layer of rock that holds water in its pores.

archipelago A group of small islands.

Arctic Circle A line of latitude that lies 66 degrees 30 minutes (66°30´) north of the equator. From September 21 to December 21, the area north of the Arctic Circle is increasingly in darkness. It has 24 hours of darkness on December 21 and then daylight begins at the Arctic Circle and moves north to the pole. On March 21 the area within the Arctic Circle has 12 hours of daylight and 12 hours of darkness. From March 21 the hours of daylight increase until the sun rises for 24 hours on June 21.

arid Land that is arid is extremely dry because very little rain has fallen on it.

arroyo A dry streambed.

art, fine Visual, literary, and movement arts that communicate what a culture finds beautiful.

atoll A horseshoe-shaped island formed by coral and surrounding a lagoon.

bank, river The land along the sides of a river or canal.

basin, river	Land drained by a river or a river system.
bay	A curved area along a coast or shore where the water juts into the land. A bay is usually smaller than a gulf and usually has a smaller opening.
bayou	A system of swampland with slow-moving streams flowing through it, found in the southern United States.
bedrock	The solid rock that lies beneath the soil on the earth's surface.
beliefs	Attitudes, ideas, and world views held by a person or group of people.
birthrate	The number of babies born alive as a proportion of the population in a specific place in a specific amount of time.
blizzard	Heavy snowfall with high wind.
bog	A small, very acidic body of water that has no natural inlets and is surrounded by rings of vegetation. A mat of grasses may grow on top. As the grasses die and build up, the bog water is replaced by a spongy mass of peat.
branch	One of the two main streams that join to form a larger river.
butte	A flat-topped hill formed when hard rock on the surface protects softer soil underneath it from being eroded. A butte is often steep sided.
canyon	A valley with very steep sides and a flat bottom, usually cut into the rock by a river. A canyon is larger than a gorge.
cape	A point of land that extends into a sea or an ocean.
chinook	A warm, dry wind that blows down the slopes of the Rocky Mountains in winter and in early spring, and melts the snow at the base of the mountains.
city	A place where a large number of people live close together; an urban area.
cliff	A high, steep rock face.

climate	The usual weather in a particular place over a period of time.
coast	The land beside a sea or ocean.
commercial area	A part of a city where business or industry is located.
continent	A large mass of land surrounded by oceans.
continental climate	A type of climate with hot summers and cold winters, common in the center of continents.
continental divide	A highland or ridge of mountains that causes rivers and streams to flow in different directions across continents, eventually reaching different oceans.
continental drift	The movement of the continents on the earth's surface.
continental shelf	The part of the continents that extends below sea level toward the deeper ocean.
core	The center part of the earth, consisting of a molten outer core and a solid inner core.
course, river	The part of a river between its source and its mouth.
crater	The cup-shaped indentation at the top of a volcano.
crevasse	A deep crack in a glacier.
crust	The outer layer of the earth.
cuisine	A particular style of preparing food.
culture	The behavior—language, beliefs, traditions, arts and crafts, political systems, and technologies— of a group of people.
current	Cold and warm "rivers" of seawater that flow in the oceans. Also, streams of cold or warm air that flow through the atmosphere.
customs	The traditions of a group of people.
cyclone	A name for various air movements involving spiral motion, including typhoon, hurricane,

and tornado. Also the common name for a hurricane-type storm in the Pacific.

delta An area of land shaped like a triangle where a river deposits mud, sand, or pebbles as it enters the sea.

desert A dry region, with fewer than 10 inches of precipitation annually.

developed country A developed country has a lot of industry and a high standard of living.

developing country A developing country has little industry and a low standard of living.

divide High land—either a hill or a mountain—that causes rivers to flow in different directions.

downstream The direction of a river's flow.

downtown The main business area of a city.

drainage The running off of rainwater from land.

drift Soil, silt, and rock deposited by a glacier.

drought An extra-long period without precipitation.

drumlin A long, narrow hill formed by glacial deposits.

dune A hill of sand formed by blowing winds.

eclipse, lunar Event that occurs when light from the sun is blocked by the earth passing between the sun and moon, so that the earth casts a shadow on the moon (see p. 14).

eclipse, solar Event that occurs when sunlight is blocked by the moon as it passes between the sun and earth, casting a shadow on the earth (see p. 14).

economy The system used by a state, region, or country to manage its industry, trade, and finance.

equator A line on a map or globe halfway between the north and south poles. The equator is almost 25,000 miles around.

escarpment A cliff or steep bank located inland rather than at the shore.

esker	A long, narrow ridge of coarse gravel deposited by a stream flowing under or through a glacier.
estuary	The part of a river affected by the tides of the sea it's about to flow into.
exurb	A sparsely populated residential area just outside the suburbs of a city.
fall line	The region where elevation drops and rivers descend over a waterfall or rapids to lower elevations.
fault	A huge crack in the earth's surface, usually caused by earth's movements.
fishery	The business of fishing; also, a fish farm.
floodplain	The low, flat area on either side of a river, which the river will flood in times of high water.
forest	A large, dense growth of trees, plants, and underbrush.
forestry	The process of growing, maintaining, and harvesting forests.
fork	A separation into two or more branches, as of a stream.
geographic grid	The intersecting pattern formed by the lines of longitude and latitude.
geographic north pole	Also true north pole. The point on the earth located at 90 degrees (90°) north latitude, where the lines of longitude meet.
geography	The study of the world, how it works, and how people use and change the world as they live in it.
geopolitical	A geopolitical map shows both political and physical features.
geyser	A spout of water heated by molten rock underground.
glacier	A thick bed of ice that covers a continent or a river of thick ice that moves slowly down a slope or valley.
globe	A sphere-shaped model of the earth.
gorge	A steep-sided, V-shaped canyon, usually caused by swiftly flowing water.

gross domestic product The total output of a country or region, including all its products and the labor of its people.

groundwater Water found beneath the earth's surface.

gulf A large area of sea that is partly surrounded by land.

headwater The source of a river or river system.

hemispheres Halves of the earth. The equator divides the earth into northern and southern hemispheres. The prime meridian and 180 degrees (180°) longitude divide the earth into eastern and western hemispheres.

hill A part of the earth's surface that rises gently above the level of the surrounding land.

humid When air is humid, it contains a lot of moisture.

humus Soil made up of decomposed animals and plants.

hurricane A violent, usually late-summer storm in the Atlantic Ocean.

iceberg A mass of floating ice broken off from a glacier. Only a small patch of an iceberg shows above water.

ice-cap climate An area with an ice-cap climate is constantly covered by snow and ice.

ice floe A sheet of floating, frozen seawater.

industry The making and selling of products.

international date line A line on a map or globe drawn from the north pole to the south pole, roughly following 180 degrees (180°) longitude, but turning and twisting to miss islands and other bodies of land. It is where the days of the week change. It is one day earlier east of the date line than it is west.

island A body of land completely surrounded by water.

isthmus A narrow strip of land that connects two larger bodies of land.

jungle A very dense tangle of tropical vegetation.

lagoon A shallow body of calm water separated from the sea by a narrow strip of land.

lake	A body of water surrounded by land. The water in lakes is usually fresh, but may be salty.
landform	Any of a number of natural features on the earth's surface, including mountains, plains, plateaus, hills, canyons, cliffs, etc.
language	The use of voice sounds, gestures, and written symbols to communicate thoughts and feelings.
leeward	Facing the direction toward which the wind is blowing.
loam	Soil that contains sand and clay as well as silt and humus.
loess	Fine soil particles and dust that are carried by the wind and water and pile up to form a rich, thick soil.
magnetic north pole	The point on the earth to which a magnetized compass needle points.
mantle	The part of earth that lies between the core and the crust.
manufacturing	The creation of products from raw and recycled materials.
map	A picture of a place drawn on a flat surface.
marine climate	A mild and wet climate usually found near the sea.
marsh	A body of moving water, fresh or salty, with reeds growing in it. A marsh is usually near a river or sea coast.
megalopolis	A group of cities whose boundaries have extended to meet each other.
mental maps	Pictures in your mind of familiar places or regions.
mesa	A hill or mountain feature with a flat top and steep sides. A mesa is larger than a butte.
metropolis	A large city.
migration, human	The movement of people from one place to another, usually for economic or political reasons.
mining	Taking minerals out of the earth.

mistral	A strong, cold, dry northerly wind that sometimes brings very cold air down the Rhone River valley in France.
monsoon	Seasonal reversal in wind direction that brings heavy rainfall in parts of southern Asia.
moraine	A mound of soil and pebbles were carried by a glacier and then dropped when the glacier receded.
mountain	A part of the land that rises abruptly to at least 1,000 feet above the surrounding land.
mouth, river	The place where a river flows into a larger body of water.
neighborhood	Area within a city or town that has a unique cultural makeup.
north pole	See geographic north pole and magnetic north pole.
oasis	A place in a desert where there is a source of water that can support some plant life.
ocean	A large body of salt water that separates continents.
oxbow	A u-shaped bend in a river.
peak	The highest point of a mountain.
peninsula	A piece of land that juts into a body of water and is surrounded by water on three sides.
permafrost	Permanently frozen subsoil.
plain	Nearly flat region of land.
plate	One of the hard sections of the earth's crust on which the continents lie.
plateau	A large, mostly level area of land that stands higher than the surrounding area. A plateau is larger than a butte.
political system	A method of government.
pond	A small body of fresh water.
population	The total number of people who live in a particular place.

population data	Facts about populations, including history, migration patterns, and current information.
population profile	A graph that shows different age groups within a population.
population pyramid	A bar graph that shows total population in terms of age and gender.
postindustrial economy	An economy that was once based on industry but is now based on services such as banking, computers, and health care.
prairie	Treeless plain, usually covered by tall grass.
precipitation	Any of the forms in which water falls on the earth's surface (rain, snow, hail, etc.).
pre-industrial economy	An economy with very little industry.
prevailing wind	The direction the wind usually blows across a particular place or region.
prime meridian	The line of longitude drawn from the north pole to the south pole at zero degrees (0°).
projections, map	Representations of the geographic grid used to make world maps.
rain forest	Forest in tropical climates with dense canopies, vines, and understories of growth.
range	A large area of open land. Animals usually graze on the grass on range lands.
range, mountain	A group or chain of mountains.
ravine	A deep, narrow canyon.
reef	A ridge of sand, coral, or bedrock under water but near the surface.
rift valley	A valley formed by the folding and the faulting of the earth's crust along parallel lines.
river	A large stream that flows from a source to a larger body of water, for example, a larger river, lake, sea, or ocean.
rural	A rural area is made up of farmland or countryside.
savanna	Tropical grassland with few trees.

sea	A large body of salt water surrounded partly by or next to land.
seamount	Underwater mountain with steep sides that rises from the ocean floor.
shore	The land beside a body of water.
silt	Fine grains of soil carried by water.
soil	Particles of bedrock, decomposed animal and plant matter, water, and air pockets that cover the earth's surface and that plants grow in.
source, river	The beginning of a river.
south pole	The point on the earth located at 90 degrees (90°) south latitude where the lines of longitude meet.
standard of living	A measurement of the availability of jobs, housing, food, and education to average citizens in a specific area or country. A high standard of living means greater availability, a low standard, lesser availability.
steppe	Any of the vast, treeless plains found in southeastern Europe and Asia.
steppe climate	Dry climate, but with greater precipitation than in a desert climate.
strait	A narrow body of water that connects two larger bodies of water.
stream	A small river.
suburb	Residential area lying just outside a city or town.
swamp	A wetland similar to a marsh but usually larger in area. It supports a wider variety of plant life, including trees and shrubs.
tableland	A plateau.
taiga	Cool, high-latitude land with low trees.
technology	The use of scientific knowledge, usually to improve industry or commerce.
tectonic plates	The pieces of the earth's crust that float on the mantel.

temperate climate	A climate without extremes of either heat or cold.
temperature	A measurement of heat.
thunderstorm	A storm accompanied by lightning, thunder, heavy rain, and sometimes hail.
tide	A change in the level of an ocean or a sea, both daily and over a year, due to the pull of gravity between the earth and the moon.
till	Soil and rock deposits spread out by a glacier as it moves on or melts.
tornado	Violent and destructive cyclone that occurs inland.
trade wind	The prevailing wind of the tropics.
tributary	A stream or river that flows into a larger stream or river.
Tropic of Cancer	A line of latitude that runs parallel to the equator. It is located at 23 degrees 30 minutes (23° 30′) north of the equator. During the summer solstice (June 21), the sun is directly overhead at the Tropic of Cancer.
Tropic of Capricorn	A line of latitude that runs parallel to the equator. It is located at 23 degrees 30 minutes (23° 30′) south of the equator. During the winter solstice (December 21), the sun is directly overhead at the Tropic of Capricorn.
tsunami	A huge wave that may sometimes move through the water faster than 400 miles an hour and reach a height of more than 100 feet.
tundra	A plain in the arctic where mosses and low-growing plants grow, but not trees.
typhoon	A violent late-summer storm in the northwest Pacific.
urban	An urban area is a city or town.
valley	A U-shaped lowland between hills or mountains.
volcano	An opening in the earth's crust from which molten rocks erupt. The rocks usually form a mountain around the opening.

watershed   Area whose rainfall runs, on the surface and as groundwater, to feed a particular river.

weather   The conditions in the earth's atmosphere at a certain place and time.

weathering   The breakdown of rock on the earth's surface due to wind, water, and chemical actions.

wind   Air moving across the earth's surface.

windward   Facing the direction from which the wind is blowing.

2. Atlas

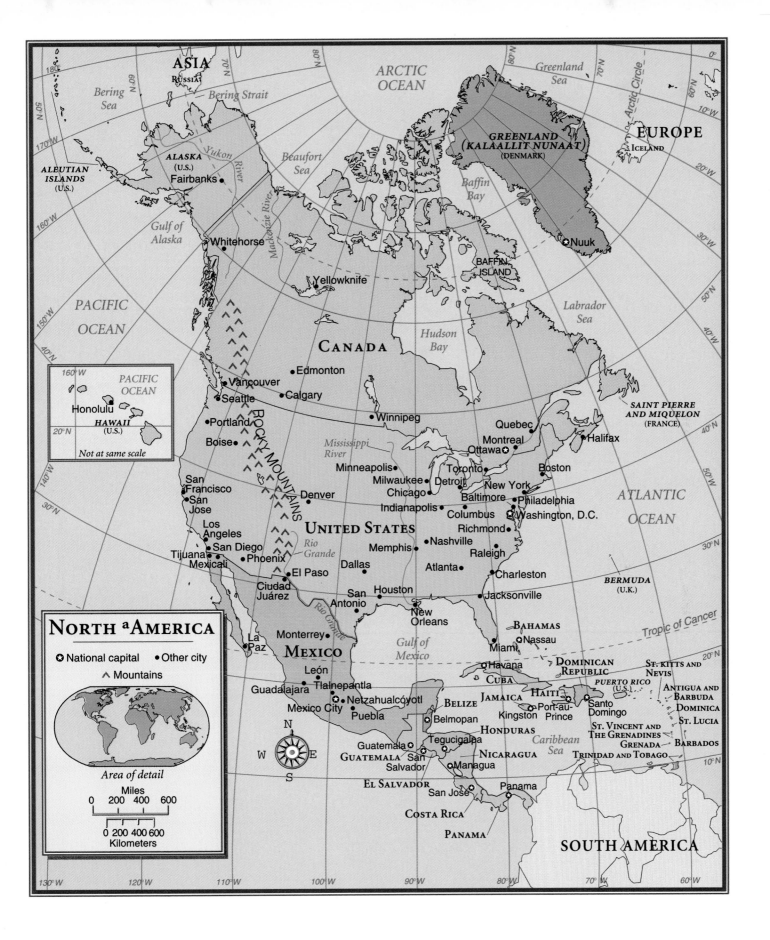

ASIA
RUSSIA
Bering Sea
Bering Strait
ARCTIC OCEAN
Greenland Sea
Arctic Circle
EUROPE
ICELAND

ALEUTIAN ISLANDS (U.S.)
ALASKA (U.S.)
Fairbanks
Yukon River
Beaufort Sea
GREENLAND (KALAALLIT NUNAAT) (DENMARK)
Baffin Bay

PACIFIC OCEAN
Gulf of Alaska
Whitehorse
Mackenzie River
Nuuk
BAFFIN ISLAND

160° W
PACIFIC OCEAN
Honolulu
HAWAII (U.S.)
20° N
Not at same scale

Yellowknife
Labrador Sea

CANADA
Hudson Bay

SAINT PIERRE AND MIQUELON (FRANCE)

Edmonton
Vancouver
Seattle
Calgary
Winnipeg
Quebec
Montreal
Halifax
Portland
Ottawa
Boise
ROCKY MOUNTAINS
Mississippi River
Minneapolis
Toronto
Boston
Milwaukee
Detroit
New York
San Francisco
Denver
Chicago
Baltimore
Philadelphia
San Jose
Indianapolis
Columbus
Washington, D.C.
ATLANTIC OCEAN
Los Angeles
UNITED STATES
Richmond
San Diego
Rio Grande
Memphis
Nashville
Raleigh
Tijuana
Phoenix
Dallas
Atlanta
Charleston
Mexicali
El Paso
BERMUDA (U.K.)
Ciudad Juárez
San Antonio
Houston
Jacksonville
Rio Grande
New Orleans
Monterrey
BAHAMAS
La Paz
Gulf of Mexico
Nassau
Tropic of Cancer
MEXICO
Miami
Havana
DOMINICAN REPUBLIC
ST. KITTS AND NEVIS
León
CUBA
PUERTO RICO (U.S.)
ANTIGUA AND BARBUDA
Guadalajara
Tlalnepantla
HAITI
DOMINICA
Netzahualcóyotl
JAMAICA
Port-au-Prince
Santo Domingo
ST. LUCIA
Mexico City
Puebla
BELIZE
Belmopan
Kingston
ST. VINCENT AND THE GRENADINES
HONDURAS
GRENADA
BARBADOS
Guatemala
Tegucigalpa
Caribbean Sea
TRINIDAD AND TOBAGO
GUATEMALA
San Salvador
NICARAGUA
Managua
EL SALVADOR
Panama
San Jose
COSTA RICA
PANAMA
SOUTH AMERICA

NORTH ᵃAMERICA
✪ National capital   • Other city
⋀ Mountains
Area of detail
Miles
0 200 400 600
0 200 400 600
Kilometers

N W E S

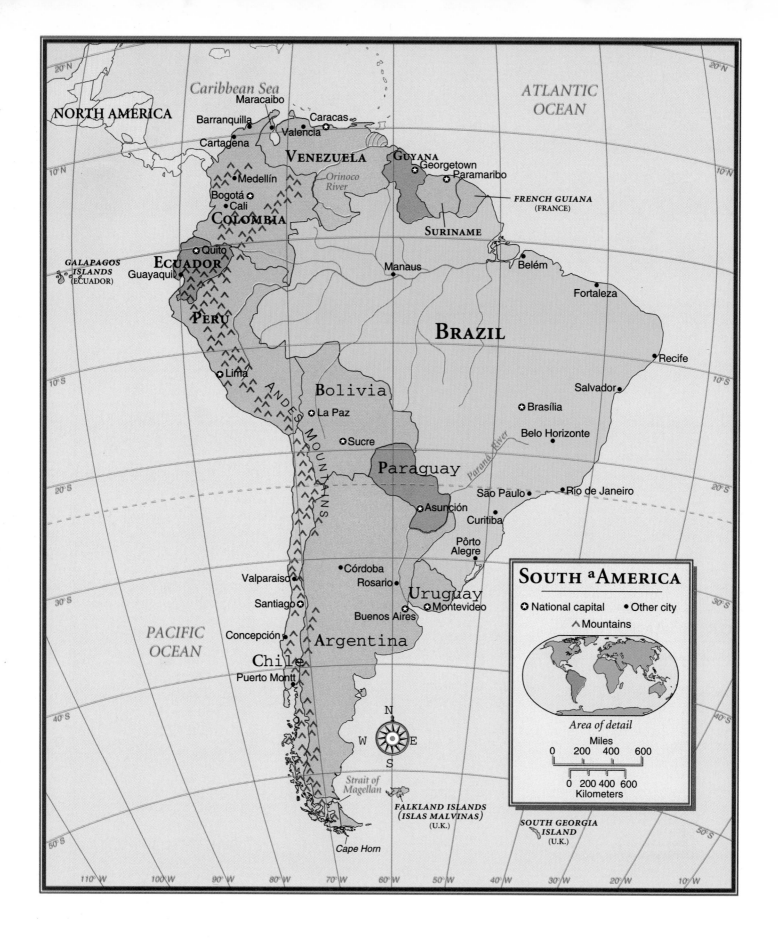

NORTH AMERICA

Caribbean Sea

ATLANTIC OCEAN

Maracaibo
Barranquilla
Caracas
Valencia
Cartagena
VENEZUELA
GUYANA
Georgetown
Paramaribo
Medellín
Orinoco River
FRENCH GUIANA (FRANCE)
Bogotá
Cali
SURINAME
COLOMBIA
Quito
GALAPAGOS ISLANDS (ECUADOR)
ECUADOR
Manaus
Belém
Guayaquil
Fortaleza
PERU
BRAZIL
Recife
Lima
Salvador
Bolivia
Brasília
La Paz
Belo Horizonte
Sucre
Paraná River
Paraguay
São Paulo
Rio de Janeiro
ANDES MOUNTAINS
Asunción
Curitiba
Pôrto Alegre
Córdoba
Valparaiso
Rosario
Uruguay
Santiago
Buenos Aires
Montevideo
PACIFIC OCEAN
Concepción
Argentina
Chile
Puerto Montt

N
W E
S

Strait of Magellan

FALKLAND ISLANDS (ISLAS MALVINAS) (U.K.)

SOUTH GEORGIA ISLAND (U.K.)

Cape Horn

SOUTH ᵃAMERICA

✪ National capital   • Other city

ᴧ Mountains

Area of detail

Miles
0   200   400   600

0   200 400 600
Kilometers

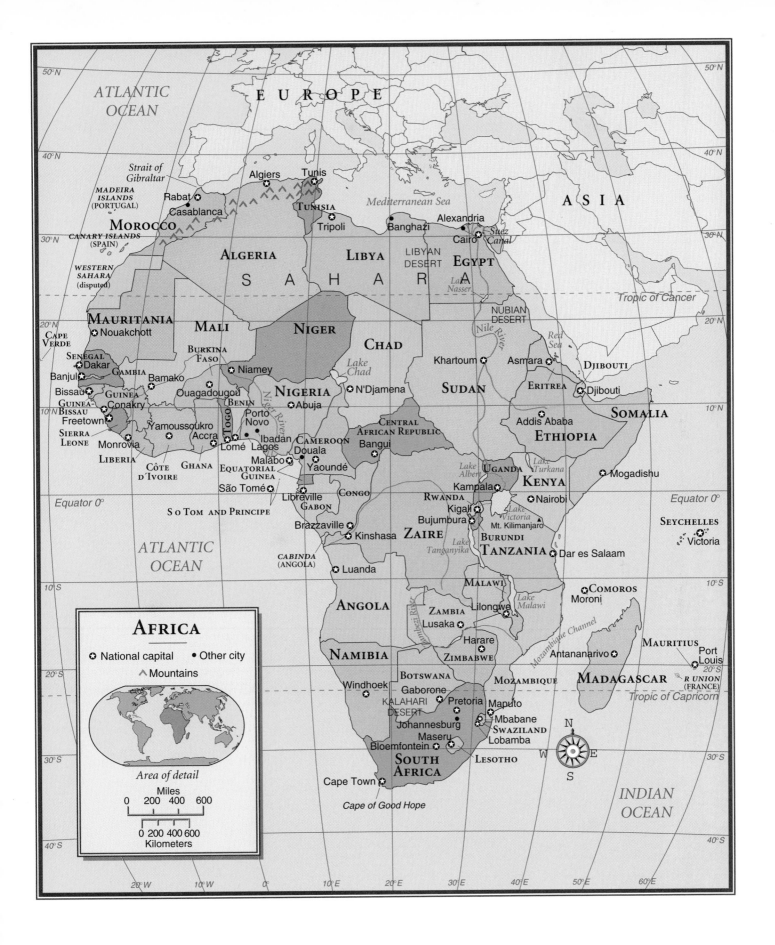

AFRICA

✪ National capital • Other city

⋀ Mountains

Area of detail

Miles
0 200 400 600

0 200 400 600
Kilometers

ATLANTIC OCEAN

E U R O P E

A S I A

Mediterranean Sea

Strait of Gibraltar

MADEIRA ISLANDS (PORTUGAL)

Algiers Tunis
Rabat
Casablanca

MOROCCO
TUNISIA
Tripoli
Banghazi
Alexandria
Cairo
Suez Canal

CANARY ISLANDS (SPAIN)

ALGERIA
LIBYA
LIBYAN DESERT
EGYPT

WESTERN SAHARA (disputed)

S A H A R A

Lake Nasser

Tropic of Cancer

CAPE VERDE

MAURITANIA
Nouakchott

MALI
NIGER
CHAD

NUBIAN DESERT

Nile River

Red Sea

Khartoum
Asmara
DJIBOUTI

BURKINA FASO

SENEGAL
Dakar
Banjul
GAMBIA
Bamako
Bissau
GUINEA
Conakry
Niamey
Lake Chad

N'Djamena

SUDAN
ERITREA
Djibouti

GUINEA BISSAU
Freetown
SIERRA LEONE
Monrovia
LIBERIA

Ouagadougou
NIGERIA
Abuja
BENIN
Porto Novo

Yamoussoukro
Accra
Lomé Lagos
Ibadan

TOGO

CENTRAL AFRICAN REPUBLIC
Bangui

Addis Ababa
ETHIOPIA

SOMALIA

Mogadishu

Côte D'Ivoire
GHANA
Malabo
EQUATORIAL GUINEA
São Tomé

CAMEROON
Douala
Yaoundé

Lake Albert
Lake Turkana

UGANDA
Kampala

KENYA
Nairobi

Niger River

Libreville
GABON
CONGO

Lake Victoria

RWANDA
Kigali
Bujumbura

Mt. Kilimanjaro

Equator 0°

SEYCHELLES
Victoria

S o Tom and Principe

Brazzaville
Kinshasa

ZAIRE

BURUNDI

TANZANIA
Dar es Salaam

Equator 0°

ATLANTIC OCEAN

CABINDA (ANGOLA)

Luanda

Lake Tanganyika

MALAWI

COMOROS
Moroni

ANGOLA

Zambezi River

ZAMBIA
Lusaka

Lilongwe
Lake Malawi

MAURITIUS
Port Louis

SEYCHELLES

Harare

Antananarivo

MADAGASCAR

NAMIBIA
ZIMBABWE

MOZAMBIQUE

R UNION (FRANCE)

Mozambique Channel

Tropic of Capricorn

Windhoek

BOTSWANA
Gaborone

KALAHARI DESERT

Pretoria
Maputo
Mbabane
SWAZILAND
Lobamba

Johannesburg
Maseru
Bloemfontein

LESOTHO

N
W E
S

SOUTH AFRICA

Cape Town

Cape of Good Hope

INDIAN OCEAN

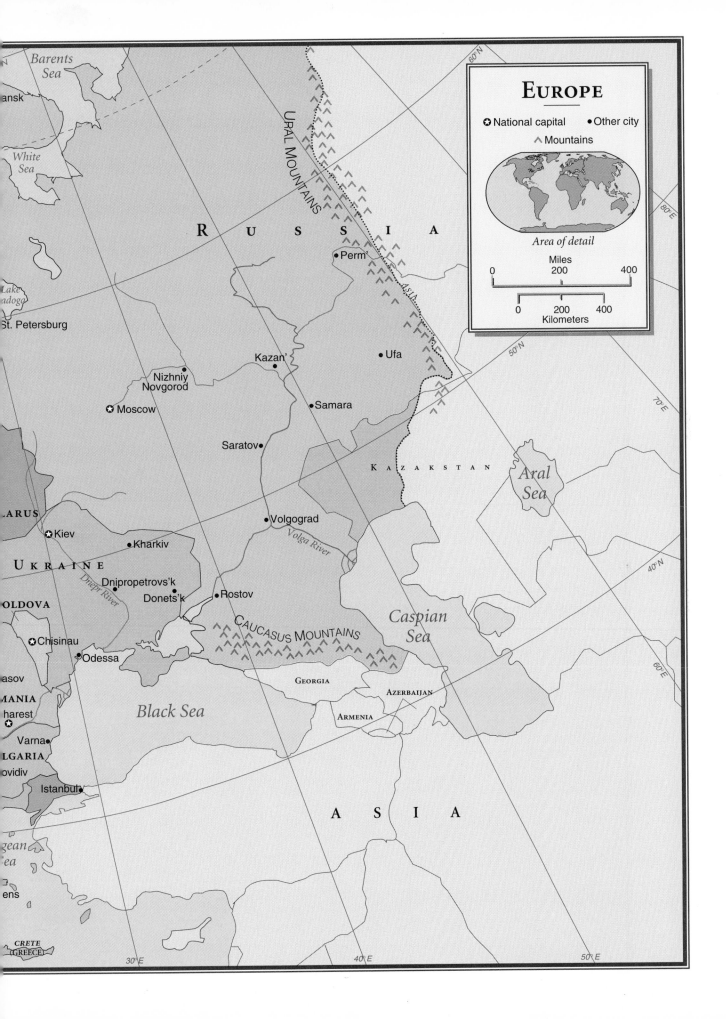

Barents Sea

White Sea

Lake Ladoga

St. Petersburg

URAL MOUNTAINS

R U S S I A

• Perm'

ASIA

Kazan' •

• Ufa

Nizhniy Novgorod •

⊛ Moscow

• Samara

Saratov •

K A Z A K S T A N

Aral Sea

• Volgograd

Volga River

LARUS

⊛ Kiev

• Kharkiv

U K R A I N E

Dnepr River

Dnipropetrovs'k •

Donets'k •

• Rostov

OLDOVA

⊛ Chisinau

• Odessa

CAUCASUS MOUNTAINS

Caspian Sea

asov

MANIA

GEORGIA

AZERBAIJAN

harest

⊛

Black Sea

ARMENIA

Varna •

LGARIA

ovidiv

Istanbul •

A S I A

gean

ea

ens

CRETE
(GREECE)

EUROPE

⊛ National capital   • Other city

∧ Mountains

Area of detail

Miles
0   200   400

0   200   400
Kilometers

60° N

80° E

50° N

70° E

40° N

60° E

30° E

40° E

50° E

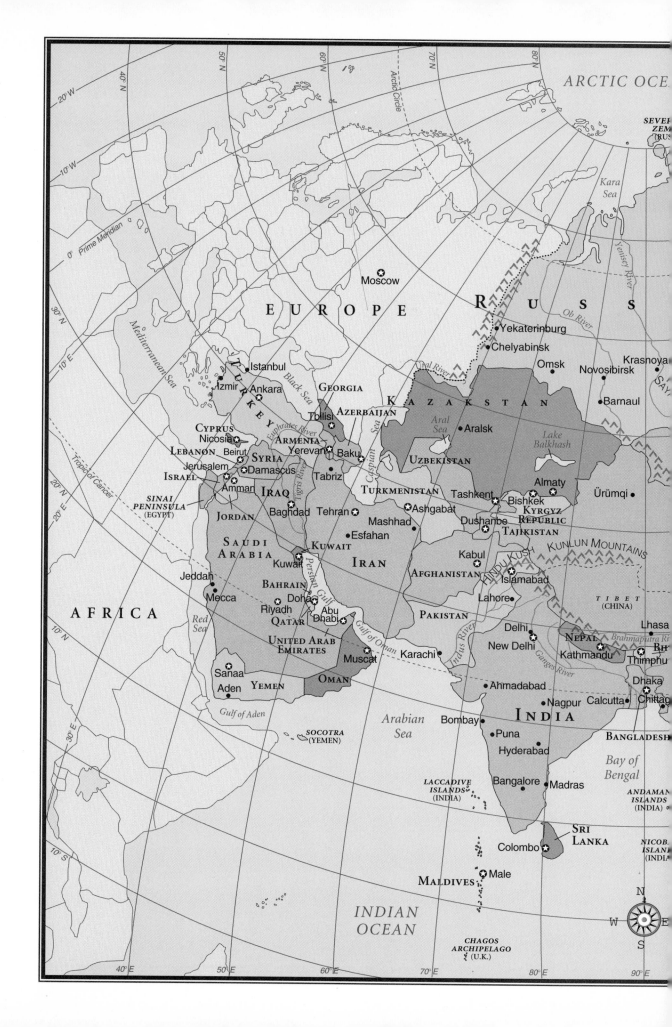

SEVER
ZEM
(RUS

Kara
Sea

Yenisey River

Moscow

E U R O P E   R U S S

Ob River

Yekaterinburg

Chelyabinsk

Omsk   Krasnoya

Novosibirsk

Barnaul

SAY

Mediterranean Sea

Istanbul

Izmir   Ankara   GEORGIA

K A Z A K S T A N

Aral
Sea   Aralsk

Lake
Balkhash

Black Sea

Tbilisi   AZERBAIJAN   K

CYPRUS
Nicosia

Euphrates River

ARMENIA
Yerevan   Baku

Caspian Sea

UZBEKISTAN

LEBANON   Beirut

SYRIA

Jerusalem   Damascus   Tabriz

ISRAEL   Amman   IRAQ

Tigris River

TURKMENISTAN   Tashkent   Bishkek
Almaty   Ürümqi

SINAI
PENINSULA
(EGYPT)

JORDAN   Baghdad   Tehran   Mashhad   Ashgabat   Dushanbe   KYRGYZ
REPUBLIC

Esfahan   TAJIKISTAN

KUNLUN MOUNTAINS

S A U D I
A R A B I A   KUWAIT

Kabul   HINDU KUSH

Kuwait   IRAN   AFGHANISTAN

Jeddah

Persian Gulf   Islamabad

Mecca   BAHRAIN   Doha   TIBET
(CHINA)

Lahore

Riyadh   Abu   Dhabi   PAKISTAN   Delhi   Lhasa

QATAR   Dhabi

Red
Sea   UNITED ARAB
EMIRATES   Gulf of Oman   Indus River   New Delhi   NEPAL   Brahmaputra Ri
BH
Kathmandu   Thimphu

Muscat   Karachi   Ganges River   Dhaka

AFRICA

Sanaa   OMAN   Ahmadabad   Chittag

Aden   YEMEN   Nagpur   Calcutta   I N D I A

Gulf of Aden   Bombay   BANGLADESH

SOCOTRA
(YEMEN)   Arabian
Sea   Puna

Hyderabad

LACCADIVE
ISLANDS
(INDIA)   Bangalore   Madras   ANDAMAN
ISLANDS
(INDIA)

SRI
LANKA   NICOB.
ISLAND
(INDIA

Colombo

MALDIVES   Male

INDIAN
OCEAN   CHAGOS
ARCHIPELAGO
(U.K.)

N
W   E
S

106

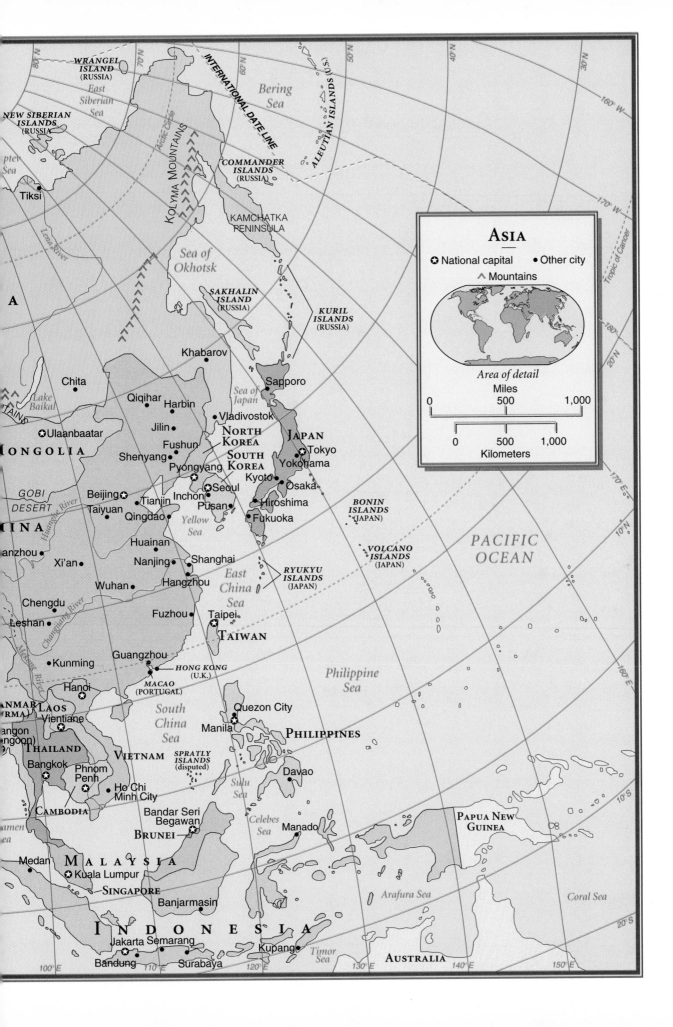

WRANGEL
ISLAND
(RUSSIA)

*East
Siberian
Sea*

INTERNATIONAL DATE LINE

*Bering
Sea*

NEW SIBERIAN
ISLANDS
(RUSSIA)

 pter
Sea

• Tiksi

KOLYMA MOUNTAINS

Arctic Circle

ALEUTIAN ISLANDS (U.S.)

COMMANDER
ISLANDS
(RUSSIA)

KAMCHATKA
PENINSULA

*Sea of
Okhotsk*

SAKHALIN
ISLAND
(RUSSIA)

KURIL
ISLANDS
(RUSSIA)

• Khabarov

• Sapporo

*Sea of
Japan*

ASIA

⊗ National capital   • Other city

⌃ Mountains

Area of detail

Miles

0   500   1,000

0   500   1,000

Kilometers

Tropic of Cancer

*Lake
Baikal*

• Chita

• Qiqihar   • Harbin

• Jilin

• Vladivostok

⊗ Ulaanbaatar

NORTH
KOREA

JAPAN

MONGOLIA

• Fushun

SOUTH
KOREA

⊗ Tokyo

• Shenyang

Pyongyang ⊗

• Yokohama

GOBI
DESERT

⊗ Beijing

⊗ Seoul

• Kyoto

• Osaka

Huanghe River

• Tianjin

Inchon •

• Hiroshima

BONIN
ISLANDS
(JAPAN)

INA

• Taiyuan

• Pusan

Yellow
Sea

• Fukuoka

anzhou

• Qingdao

CHINA

• Huainan

Changjiang River

• Xi'an

• Nanjing

• Shanghai

VOLCANO
ISLANDS
(JAPAN)

• Wuhan

• Hangzhou

*East
China
Sea*

RYUKYU
ISLANDS
(JAPAN)

*PACIFIC
OCEAN*

• Chengdu

Mekong River

• Leshan

• Fuzhou

⊗ Taipei

TAIWAN

• Kunming

• Guangzhou

HONG KONG
(U.K.)

*Philippine
Sea*

• Hanoi

MACAO
(PORTUGAL)

amen
ea

NMAR
RMA)

LAOS

• Vientiane

*South
China
Sea*

⊗ Quezon City

• Manila

PHILIPPINES

angon
ngoon)

THAILAND

VIETNAM

SPRATLY
ISLANDS
(disputed)

• Davao

⊗ Bangkok

⊗ Phnom
Penh

• Ho Chi
Minh City

*Sulu
Sea*

CAMBODIA

Bandar Seri
Begawan

*Celebes
Sea*

• Manado

PAPUA NEW
GUINEA

BRUNEI ⊗

• Medan

MALAYSIA

⊗ Kuala Lumpur

SINGAPORE

Arafura Sea

Coral Sea

• Banjarmasin

INDONESIA

Jakarta Semarang

• Kupang

*Timor
Sea*

AUSTRALIA

• Bandung   • Surabaya

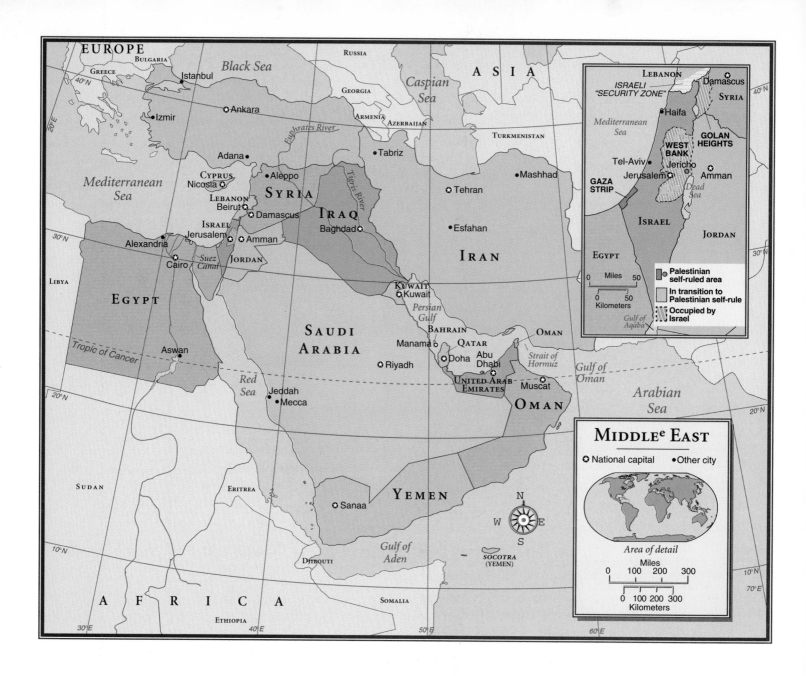

EUROPE

GREECE

BULGARIA

*Istanbul

Black Sea

RUSSIA

ASIA

Caspian Sea

GEORGIA

•Izmir

*Ankara

ARMENIA

AZERBAIJAN

TURKMENISTAN

40°N

Euphrates River

•Tabriz

•Adana

CYPRUS

Mediterranean Sea

Nicosia

•Aleppo

SYRIA

Tigris River

•Mashhad

LEBANON

Damascus

Beirut

IRAQ

*Tehran

ISRAEL

Jerusalem

•Damascus

Baghdad

Alexandria

Amman

30°N

IRAN

•Esfahan

Cairo

Suez Canal

JORDAN

LIBYA

KUWAIT

EGYPT

Kuwait

Persian Gulf

BAHRAIN

OMAN

Tropic of Cancer

SAUDI ARABIA

Manama

QATAR

Aswan

Doha

Abu Dhabi

Strait of Hormuz

Gulf of Oman

•Riyadh

UNITED ARAB EMIRATES

20°N

Red Sea

Muscat

Jeddah

OMAN

Arabian Sea

•Mecca

SUDAN

ERITREA

YEMEN

N

Sanaa

W   E

DJIBOUTI

Gulf of Aden

S

SOCOTRA (YEMEN)

10°N

AFRICA

ETHIOPIA

SOMALIA

30°E

40°E

50°E

60°E

70°E

LEBANON

ISRAELI "SECURITY ZONE"

Damascus

SYRIA

40°N

Mediterranean Sea

*Haifa

GOLAN HEIGHTS

WEST BANK

Tel-Aviv

Jericho

*Amman

GAZA STRIP

Jerusalem

ISRAEL

Dead Sea

JORDAN

EGYPT

30°N

0   Miles   50

Palestinian self-ruled area

In transition to Palestinian self-rule

Occupied by Israel

0 50
Kilometers

Gulf of Aqaba

MIDDLEᵉ EAST

National capital   Other city

Area of detail

Miles
0   100   200   300

0 100 200 300
Kilometers

108

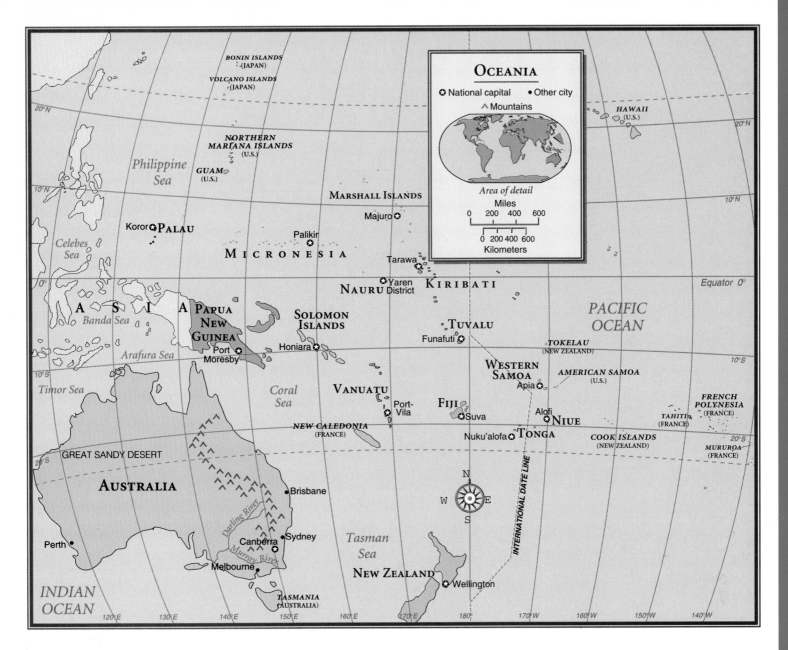

BONIN ISLANDS
(JAPAN)

VOLCANO ISLANDS
(JAPAN)

*Philippine
Sea*

HAWAII
(U.S.)

20° N

10° N

NORTHERN
MARIANA ISLANDS
(U.S.)

GUAM
(U.S.)

MARSHALL ISLANDS

Majuro

OCEANIA

✪ National capital   ● Other city

⌃ Mountains

Area of detail

Miles

0   200   400   600

0 200 400 600
Kilometers

Koror ✪ PALAU

*Celebes
Sea*

Palikir ✪

MICRONESIA

Tarawa

Yaren ✪
District

KIRIBATI

Equator 0°

10° N

0°

ASIA

Banda Sea

PAPUA
NEW
GUINEA

SOLOMON
ISLANDS

TUVALU

Funafuti ✪

TOKELAU
(NEW ZEALAND)

PACIFIC
OCEAN

Arafura Sea

Port ✪
Moresby

Honiara ✪

WESTERN
SAMOA

Apia ✪

AMERICAN SAMOA
(U.S.)

10° S

10° S

Timor Sea

*Coral
Sea*

VANUATU

Port-
Vila ✪

FIJI

Suva

Alofi ✪
NIUE

FRENCH
POLYNESIA
(FRANCE)

TAHITI
(FRANCE)

NEW CALEDONIA
(FRANCE)

Nuku'alofa ✪ TONGA

COOK ISLANDS
(NEW ZEALAND)

MURUROA
(FRANCE)

20° S

GREAT SANDY DESERT

20° S

AUSTRALIA

Brisbane

Darling River

Perth

Canberra

Sydney

Murray River

Melbourne

*Tasman
Sea*

N
W   E
S

INTERNATIONAL DATE LINE

INDIAN
OCEAN

TASMANIA
(AUSTRALIA)

NEW ZEALAND

Wellington

120° E   130° E   140° E   150° E   160° E   170° E   180°   170° W   160° W   150° W   140° W

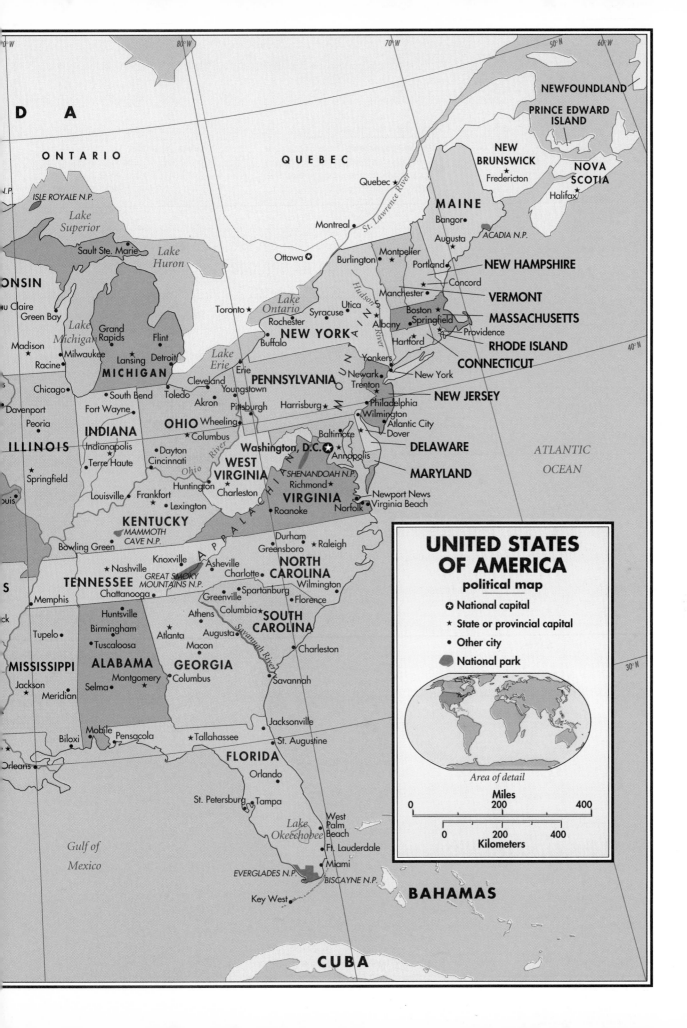

UNITED STATES OF AMERICA
political map

⊕ National capital

★ State or provincial capital

• Other city

National park

Area of detail

Miles

0   200   400

0   200   400

Kilometers

THE WORLD IN FOCUS

If you wanted to go where the people speak Trukese, what country would you visit? Where will you find no head of government, just rival warlords battling for control? Can you name the country that has been independent since the year 301? How many countries have more than one capital city?

These tables make it easy for you to find the answers to those questions and many others about the world. Before you dive into the tables, check out the example at right. It explains the kinds of data you will find here.

Area and population: The size of a country and the number of its people. Divide population by area to get the **population density** (number of people per square mile).

Urban population: This number is the percentage of a country's total population living in urban areas. (To get the rural population, subtract this figure from 100.)

Mexico	736,950	71	Mexico City
	94,800,000	2.2	

Population annual rise: This number shows the percentage of the increase in a country's population in one year. Countries with high figures may face many problems.

Major languages spoken: Noting the languages spoken by a country's people may give you insights into how it was settled and where its people come from.

Data compiled and edited by Bryan Brown, Kathy Wilmore, and Karen Peart

COUNTRY	AREA (SQ MI) / POPULATION	URBAN POP. (%) / POP. ANNUAL RISE (%)	CAPITAL	MAJOR LANGUAGES	FORM OF GOVERNMENT[1] AND HEAD	DATE OF INDEP.[2] / % OF POP. UNDER 15 YEARS	LITERACY RATE (%)[3] / LIFE EXPEC-TANCY	PER-CAPITA GDP[4] / HDI[5]
A-D								
Afghanistan	251,770 / 21,500,000	18 / 2.8	Kabul	Pashtu, Afghan Persian, Turkic languages, others	Rival warlords; President Burhanuddin Rabbani	1919 / 41	44/14 / 43/44	NA / 0.23
Albania	10,580 / 3,300,000	37 / 1.7	Tiranë	Albanian, Greek	Presidential-parliamentary democracy; Prime Minister Alexander Meksi	1912 / 33	80/63 / 70/76	$1,110 / 0.63
Algeria	919,590 / 29,000,000	50 / 2.4	Algiers	Arabic, French, Berber dialects	Military; President Liamine Zeroual	1962 / 40	70/46 / 67/68	$3,480 / 0.75
Andorra	175 / 63,930	65 / 3.0	Andorra la Vella	Catalan, French, Castilian	Parliamentary democracy; Executive Council President Marc Forne	1278 / NA	99 / 76/82	$14,000 / NA
Angola	481,350 / 11,500,000	32 / 2.7	Luanda	Portuguese, Bantu, others	Transitional; President José Eduardo dos Santos	1975 / 45	56/28 / 44/48	$620 / 0.28
Antigua and Barbuda	170 / 100,000	31 / 1.2	St. John's	English, local dialects	Dominant party; Prime Minister Lester Bird	1981 / 25	90/88 / 71/75	$6,000 / 0.87
Argentina	1,056,640 / 34,700,000	87 / 1.2	Buenos Aires	Spanish, English, Italian, German, French	Presidential-legislative democracy; President Carlos Saúl Menem	1816 / 31	96/95 / 69/76	$7,990 / 0.89
Armenia	10,890 / 3,800,000	69 / 0.7	Yerevan	Armenian, Russian, others	Dominant party; President Levon Ter-Petrosyan	1991 / 31	99/98 / 68/74	$2,290 / 0.68
Australia	2,941,290 / 18,300,000	85 / 0.8	Canberra	English, Aboriginal languages	Parliamentary democracy; Prime Minister John Howard	1901 / 21	100 / 75/81	$20,720 / 0.93
Austria	31,940 / 8,100,000	65 / 0.1	Vienna	German	Parliamentary democracy; Chancellor Franz Vranitzky	1918 / 18	99 / 73/80	$17,500 / 0.93
Azerbaijan	33,400 / 7,600,000	53 / 1.4	Baku	Azeri, Russian, Armenian, others	Dominant party; President Gaidar Aliyev	1991 / 33	100 / 66/75	$1,790 / 0.67
Bahamas	3,860 / 300,000	84 / 1.3	Nassau	English, Creole	Parliamentary democracy; Prime Minister Hubert Ingraham	1973 / 29	90/89 / 68/75	$15,900 / 0.90

FAST FACTS ON 193 COUNTRIES

Form of government and head: This describes the type of government and gives the title and name of the person who heads it.

Literacy rate: This is the percentage of people who can read and write. A single number is the percentage for the country as a whole. Two numbers divided by a slash are for male/female.

Per-capita GDP: The value of all goods and services produced within a country in one year (its gross domestic product), divided by its population. (*Per-capita* means *per-person*.)

Spanish, Indian languages	Dominant party; President Ernesto Zedillo Ponce de Léon	1810	90/85	$7,900
		36	70/76	0.85

Percent of population under age 15: Developing countries with a high percentage of young people may have trouble providing a job for everyone who wants one.

Life expectancy: This is the number of years of life expected at birth. The first number is the life expectancy for males; the second, for females.

HDI (Human Development Index): Use this number—which is calculated using life expectancy, adult literacy rate, and purchasing power—to help you compare one country's quality of life with others'.

COUNTRY	AREA (SQ MI) / POPULATION	URBAN POP. (%) / POP. ANNUAL RISE (%)	CAPITAL	MAJOR LANGUAGES	FORM OF GOVERNMENT[1] AND HEAD	DATE OF INDEP.[2] / % OF POP. UNDER 15 YEARS	LITERACY RATE (%)[3] / LIFE EXPEC-TANCY	PER-CAPITA GDP[4] / HDI[5]
Bahrain	260 / 600,000	88 / 2.6	Manama	Arabic, English, Farsi, Urdu	Monarchy; Amir Isa ibn Salman Al Khalifa	1971 / 32	89/77 / 71/76	$12,100 / 0.87
Bangladesh	50,260 / 119,800,000	16 / 2.0	Dhaka	Bangla, English	Parliamentary democracy; Sheikh Hasina Wajed	1971 / 40	47/22 / 57/57	$1,040 / 0.37
Barbados	170 / 300,000	38 / 0.5	Bridgetown	English	Parliamentary democracy; Prime Minister Owen Arthur	1966 / 24	99/99 / 73/78	$9,200 / 0.91
Belarus	80,200 / 10,300,000	69 / -0.3	Minsk	Byelorussian, Russian, others	Presidential dictatorship; President Aleksandr Lukashenko	1991 / 22	99/96 / 64/74	$5,130 / 0.79
Belgium	11,750 / 10,200,000	97 / 0.1	Brussels	Dutch, French, German, Italian	Parliamentary democracy; Premier Jean-Luc Dehaene	1830 / 18	99 / 73/80	$18,040 / 0.93
Belize	8,800 / 200,000	48 / 3.3	Belmopan	English, Spanish, Maya, Garifuna	Parliamentary democracy; Prime Minister Manuel Esquivel	1981 / 44	91/91 / 70/74	$2,750 / 0.75
Benin	42,710 / 5,600,000	36 / 3.1	Porto-Novo	French, Fon, Yoruba, others	Presidential-parliamentary democracy; President Mathieu Kérékou	1960 / 47	32/16 / 46/49	$1,260 / 0.33
Bhutan	18,150 / 800,000	17 / 2.3	Thimphu	Dzongkha; Tibetan and Nepalese dialects	Monarchy; King Jigme Singye Wangchuck	1949 / 39	NA / 51/50	$700 / 0.31
Bolivia	418,680 / 7,600,000	58 / 2.6	La Paz and Sucre	Spanish, Quechua, Aymara	Presidential-legislative democracy; President Gonzalo Sánchez de Lozada	1825 / 41	88/72 / 59/62	$2,370 / 0.58
Bosnia and Herzevogina	19,740 / 3,600,000	NA / 0.6	Sarajevo	Serbo-Croatian	Presidential-parliamentary democracy; Chairman of the Presidency Alija Izetbegovic[6]	1992 / 23	NA / 70/75	NA / NA
Botswana	218,810 / 1,500,000	46 / 2.7	Gaborone	English, Setswana	Parliamentary democracy; President Sir Ketumile Masire	1966 / 43	32/16 / 64/71	$3,130 / 0.74
Brazil	3,265,060 / 160,500,000	76 / 1.7	Brasília	Portuguese, Spanish, English, French	Presidential-legislative democracy; President Fernando Henrique Cardoso	1822 / 34	80/80 / 64/69	$5,580 / 0.80
Brunei	2,030 / 300,000	67 / 2.4	Bandar Seri Begawan	Malay, English, Chinese	Monarchy; Sultan and Prime Minister Hassanal Bolkiah Mu'izzadin Waddaulah	1984 / 35	92/82 / 73/76	$16,000 / 0.87

COUNTRY	AREA (SQ MI) / POPULATION	URBAN POP. (%) / POP. ANNUAL RISE (%)	CAPITAL	MAJOR LANGUAGES	FORM OF GOVERNMENT[1] AND HEAD	DATE OF INDEP.[2] / % OF POP. UNDER 15 YEARS	LITERACY RATE (%)[3] / LIFE EXPECTANCY	PER-CAPITA GDP[4] / HDI[5]
Bulgaria	42,680 / 8,400,000	68 / -0.4	Sofia	Bulgarian, others	Parliamentary democracy; Prime Minister Zhan Videnov	1908 / 19	99/97 / 68/75	$3,830 / 0.77
Burkino Faso	105,710 / 10,600,000	15 / 2.8	Ouagadougou	French, Sudanic languages	Dominant party; President Captain Blaise Compaoré	1960 / 48	28/9 / 44/46	$660 / 0.23
Burundi	9,900 / 5,900,000	6 / 3.0	Bujumbura	Kirundi, French, Swahili	Civilian-military; President Sylvestre Ntibantunganya	1962 / 46	61/40 / 48/52	$600 / 0.28
Cambodia	68,150 / 10,900,000	13 / 2.9	Phnom Penh	Khmer, French	Constitutional monarchy; Prime Ministers Norodom Ranariddh (1st) & Hun Sen (2nd)	1949 / 46	48/22 / 48/51	$630 / 0.33
Cameroon	179,690 / 13,600,000	41 / 2.9	Yaoundé	English, French, African languages	Dominant party; President Paul Biya	1960 / 44	66/45 / 55/58	$1,200 / 0.48
Canada	3,560,220 / 30,000,000	77 / 0.6	Ottawa	English, French	Parliamentary democracy; Prime Minister Jean Chrétien	1867 / 21	97 / 74/81	$22,760 / 0.95
Cape Verde	1,560 / 400,000	44 / 1.9	Praia	Portuguese, Crioulo	Presidential-parliamentary democracy; Prime Minister Carlos Veiga	1975 / 45	75/53 / 64/66	$1,070 / 0.54
Central African Republic	240,530 / 3,600,000	39 / 2.5	Bangui	French, Sangho, Arabic, Hunsa, Swahili	Presidential-parliamentary democracy; President Ange-Felix Patasse	1960 / 43	52/25 / 47/52	$700 / 0.36
Chad	486,180 / 6,500,000	22 / 2.6	N'Djamena	French, Arabic, Sara, others	Transitional; President Lieutenant General Idriss Deby	1960 / 41	42/18 / 46/49	$530 / 0.29
Chile	289,110 / 14,500,000	85 / 1.6	Santiago	Spanish	Presidential-legislative democracy; President Eduardo Frei	1810 / 30	95/94 / 69/76	$7,010 / 0.88
China	3,600,930 / 1,217,600,000	29 / 1.1	Beijing	Mandarin, other Chinese languages	Communist; President Jiang Zemin	1949 / 27	87/68 / 68/72	$2,500 / 0.61
Colombia	401,040 / 38,000,000	67 / 2.1	Bogotá	Spanish	Presidential-legislative democracy; President Ernesto Samper	1810 / 33	88/88 / 66/72	$4,850 / 0.84
Comoros	860 / 600,000	29 / 3.6	Moroni	Arabic, French, Comoran	Dominant party; Prime Minister Tadjidine Ben Said Massounei	1975 / 48	56/40 / 56/60	$700 / 0.40
Congo	131,850 / 2,500,000	58 / 2.3	Brazzaville	French, Lingala, Kikongo, others	Presidential-parliamentary democracy; President Pascal Lissouba	1960 / 44	71/49 / 44/48	$2,820 / 0.52
Costa Rica	19,710 / 3,600,000	44 / 2.2	San José	Spanish, English	Presidential-legislative democracy; President José Maria Figueres	1821 / 34	93/93 / 74/79	$5,050 / 0.88
Côte d'Ivoire	122,780 / 14,700,000	46 / 3.5	Yamoussoukro	French, Dioula, others	Dominant party; President Henri Konan Bédié	1960 / 47	44/23 / 50/52	$1,430 / 0.36
Croatia	21,830 / 4,400,000	54 / -0.0	Zagreb	Serbo-Croatian, others	Presidential-parliamentary democracy; President Franjo Tudjman	1991 / 20	99/95 / 66/75	$2,640 / NA
Cuba	42,400 / 11,000,000	74 / 0.7	Havana	Spanish	Communist; President Fidel Castro Ruz	1902 / 22	98 / 73/77	$1,260 / 0.73
Cyprus	3,570 / 700,000	53 / 0.9	Nicosia	Greek, Turkish, English	Presidential-legislative democracy; President Glafcos Clerides	1960 / 25	98/91 / 75/79	NA / 0.91
Czech Republc	30,590 / 10,300,000	75 / -0.1	Prague	Czech, Slovak	Parliamentary democracy; Prime Minister Vaclav Klaus	1993 / 19	99 / 70/77	$7,350 / 0.87
Denmark	16,360 / 5,200,000	85 / 0.2	Copenhagen	Danish, Faroese, Greenlandic	Parliamentary democracy; Prime Minister Poul Nyrup Rasmussen	1849 / 17	99 / 73/78	$19,860 / 0.92
Djibouti	8,950 / 600,000	77 / 2.2	Djibouti	French, Arabic, Somali, Afar	Dominant party; President Hassan Gouled Aptidon	1977 / 41	63/34 / 47/50	$1,200 / 0.29

COUNTRY	AREA (SQ MI) / POPULATION	URBAN POP. (%) / POP. ANNUAL RISE (%)	CAPITAL	MAJOR LANGUAGES	FORM OF GOVERNMENT[1] AND HEAD	DATE OF INDEP.[2] / % OF POP. UNDER 15 YEARS	LITERACY RATE (%)[3] / LIFE EXPECTANCY	PER-CAPITA GDP[4] / HDI[5]
Dominica	290 / 100,000	61 / 1.3	Roseau	English, French patois	Parliamentary democracy; Prime Minister Edison James	1978 / 32	94/94 / 74/80	$2,260 / 0.76
Dominican Republic	18,680 / 8,100,000	61 / 2.3	Santo Domingo	Spanish	Presidential-legislative democracy; President Joaquín Balaguer Ricardo	1844 / 37	85/82 / 66/71	$3,070 / 0.70

E-L

COUNTRY	AREA (SQ MI) / POPULATION	URBAN POP. (%) / POP. ANNUAL RISE (%)	CAPITAL	MAJOR LANGUAGES	FORM OF GOVERNMENT[1] AND HEAD	DATE OF INDEP.[2] / % OF POP. UNDER 15 YEARS	LITERACY RATE (%)[3] / LIFE EXPECTANCY	PER-CAPITA GDP[4] / HDI[5]
Ecuador	106,890 / 11,700,000	59 / 2.3	Quito	Spanish, Quechua, others	Presidential-legislative democracy; President Sixto Duran Ballen Cordovez	1822 / 36	90/84 / 66/71	$3,840 / 0.76
Egypt	384,340 / 63,700,000	44 / 2.2	Cairo	Arabic, English, French	Dominant party; President Hosni Mubarak	1922 / 40	63/34 / 62/65	$2,490 / 0.61
El Salvador	8,000 / 5,900,000	45 / 2.6	San Salvador	Spanish, Nahua	Presidential-legislative democracy; President Armando Calderón Sol	1821 / 40	76/70 / 65/70	$1,710 / 0.58
Equatorial Guinea	10,830 / 400,000	37 / 2.6	Malabo	Spanish, pidgin English, Fang, Bubi, Ibo	Dominant party; President Brigadier General Teodoro Obiang Nguema Mbasogo	1968 / 43	77/48 / 50/54	$700 / 0.46
Eritrea	48,260 / 3,600,000	17 / 2.8	Asmara	Tigre, Kunama, Cushitic dialects	One-party (transitional); President Issaias Afeworke	1993 / 44	NA / 49/52	$500 / NA
Estonia	17,410 / 1,500,000	70 / -0.5	Tallinn	Estonian, Latvian, Lithuanian, Russian, others	Presidential-parliamentary democracy; Prime Minister Tiit Vahi	1991 / 20	100 / 64/75	$6,460 / 0.75
Ethiopia	376,830 / 57,200,000	15 / 3.1	Addis Ababa	Amharic, Tigrinya, Orominga, others	Dominant party; Prime Minister Meles Zenawi	200 / 49	33/16 / 48/52	$380 / 0.24
Fiji	7,050 / 800,000	39 / 2.0	Suva	English, Fijian, Hindustani	Parliamentary democracy; Prime Minister Sitiveni Rabuka	1970 / 38	90/84 / 61/65	$5,650 / 0.85
Finland	117,610 / 5,100,000	64 / 0.3	Helsinki	Finnish, Swedish, Lapp, Russian	Presidential-parliamentary democracy; President Martti Ahtisaari	1917 / 19	100 / 73/80	$16,140 / 0.94
France	212,390 / 58,400,000	74 / 0.3	Paris	French, regional dialects	Presidential-parliamentary democracy; President Jacques Chirac	1792 / 20	99 / 74/82	$18,670 / 0.94
Gabon	99,490 / 1,200,000	73 / 1.5	Libreville	French, Fang, Myene, others	Dominant party; President Omar Bongo	1960 / 34	74/48 / 52/58	$4,900 / 0.56
Gambia	3,860 / 1,200,000	26 / 2.7	Banjul	English, Mandinka, Wolof, Fula, others	Military; Captain Yahya Jammeh	1965 / 45	39/16 / 48/52	$1,050 / 0.30
Georgia	26,910 / 5,400,000	56 / 0.2	Tbilisi	Georgian, Russian, Armenian, Azeri	Presidential-parliamentary democracy; Chairman of Parliament Eduard A. Shevardnadze	1991 / 24	100/98 / 69/76	$1,060 / 0.65
Germany	134,930 / 81,700,000	85 / -0.1	Berlin	German	Parliamentary democracy; Chancellor Helmut Kohl	1990 / 16	99 / 72/79	$16,580 / 0.92
Ghana	88,810 / 18,000,000	36 / 3.0	Accra	English, Akan, others	Dominant party; President Jerry John Rawlings	1957 / 45	70/51 / 54/58	$1,310 / 0.47
Greece	50,520 / 10,500,000	72 / 0.1	Athens	Greek, English, French	Parliamentary democracy; Prime Minister Konstandinos Simitif	1829 / 18	98/93 / 75/80	$8,870 / 0.90
Grenada	130 / 100,000	NA / 2.4	St. George's	English, French patois	Parliamentary democracy; Prime Minister Keith Mitchell	1974 / 43	98/98 / 68/73	$2,750 / 0.73
Guatemala	41,860 / 9,900,000	39 / 2.9	Guatemala	Spanish, Indian languages	Presidential-legislative democracy with strong military influence; President Alvaro Arzú	1821 / 45	63/47 / 62/67	$3,080 / 0.58
Guinea	94,930 / 7,400,000	29 / 2.4	Conakry	French, various African languages	Dominant party; President General Lansana Conté	1958 / 44	35/13 / 42/46	$980 / 0.31

COUNTRY	AREA (SQ MI) POPULATION	URBAN POP. (%) POP. ANNUAL RISE (%)	CAPITAL	MAJOR LANGUAGES	FORM OF GOVERNMENT[1] AND HEAD	DATE OF INDEP.[2] % OF POP. UNDER 15 YEARS	LITERACY RATE (%)[3] LIFE EXPEC- TANCY	PER-CAPITA GDP[4] HDI[5]
Guinea-Bissau	10,860 / 1,100,000	22 / 2.1	Bissau	Portuguese, Criolo, others	Presidential-parliamentary democracy; President General João Bernardo Vieira	1974 / 43	50/24 / 42/45	$840 / 0.30
Guyana	76,000 / 700,000	33 / 1.8	Georgetown	English, Amerindian languages	Parliamentary democracy; President Cheddi Jagan	1966 / 38	98/95 / 62/68	$1,950 / 0.63
Haiti	10,640 / 7,300,000	32 / 2.3	Port-au-Prince	Creole, French	Presidential-parliamentary democracy; President Rene Préval	1804 / 40	37/32 / 55/58	$870 / 0.36
Honduras	43,200 / 5,600,000	47 / 2.8	Tegucigalpa	Spanish, Indian languages	Presidential-legislative democracy; President Carlos Roberto Reina	1821 / 45	76/71 / 66/71	$1,820 / 0.58
Hungary	35,650 / 10,200,000	64 / -0.3	Budapest	Hungarian, others	Parliamentary democracy; Prime Minister Gyula Horn	1001 / 18	99/98 / 65/74	$5,700 / 0.86
Iceland	38,710 / 300,000	91 / 1.0	Reykjavík	Icelandic	Parliamentary democracy; Prime Minister David Oddsson	1944 / 25	100 / 77/81	$17,250 / 0.93
India	1,147,950 / 949,600,000	26 / 1.9	New Delhi	Hindi, English, many others	Parliamentary democracy; Prime Minister H. D. Deve Gowda	1947 / 36	64/39 / 58/59	$1,360 / 0.44
Indonesia	705,190 / 201,400,000	31 / 1.6	Jakarta	Bahasa Indonesian, others	Dominant party; President General Suharto	1945 / 35	88/75 / 61/65	$3,090 / 0.64
Iran	631,660 / 63,100,000	58 / 2.9	Tehran	Persian, Turkic, Kurdish, Luri, others	Presidential-parliamentary under religious control; President Hashemi Rafsanjani	1979 / 44	74/56 / 65/68	$4,720 / 0.75
Iraq	168,870 / 21,400,000	70 / 3.7	Baghdad	Arabic, Kurdish, Assyrian, Armenian	One-party; President Saddam Hussein	1932 / 47	90/88 / 65/67	NA / 0.60
Ireland	26,600 / 3,600,000	57 / 0.5	Dublin	English, Gaelic	Parliamentary democracy; Prime Minister John Bruton	1921 / 25	98 / 74/79	$14,060 / 0.92
Israel[7]	7,850 / 5,800,000	90 / 1.5	Jerusalem	Hebrew, Arabic, English	Parliamentary democracy; Prime Minister Benjamin Netanyahu	1948 / 30	97/93 / 75/79	$13,880 / 0.91
Italy	113,540 / 57,300,000	68 / -0.0	Rome	Italian, others	Parliamentary democracy; Prime Minister Oscar Luigi Scalfaro	1861 / 15	98/96 / 74/80	$17,180 / 0.91
Jamaica	4,180 / 2,600,000	53 / 1.8	Kingston	English, Creole	Parliamentary democracy; Prime Minister P. J. Patterson	1962 / 34	77/86 / 71/76	$3,050 / 0.70
Japan	145,370 / 125,800,000	78 / 0.2	Tokyo	Japanese	Parliamentary democracy; Prime Minister Ryutaro Hashimoto	660 B.C. / 16	99 / 77/83	$20,200 / 0.94
Jordan	34,340 / 4,200,000	78 / 2.6	Amman	Arabic, English	Constitutional monarchy; King Hussein I	1946 / 42	91/75 / 66/70	$4,280 / 0.74
Kazakstan	1,049,150 / 16,500,000	56 / 0.9	Almaty	Kazak, Russian	Dominant party; President Nursultan Nazarbayev	1991 / 31	99/96 / 64/73	$3,200 / 0.74
Kenya	219,960 / 28,200,000	27 / 2.7	Nairobi	English, Swahili, others	Dominant party; President Daniel arap Moi	1963 / 48	81/62 / 49/52	$1,170 / 0.47
Kiribati	280 / 77,853	NA / 2.0	Tarawa	English, Gilbertese	Parliamentary democracy; President Teburoro Tito	1979 / NA	NA / 53/56	$800 / NA
Korea, North	46,490 / 23,900,000	61 / 1.8	Pyongyang	Korean	Communist; President Kim Jong Il	1948 / 29	99/99 / 67/73	$920 / 0.71
Korea, South	38,120 / 45,300,000	74 / 0.9	Seoul	Korean, English	Presidential-parliamentary democracy; President Kim Young Sam	1948 / 23	99/94 / 68/76	$11,270 / 0.87
Kuwait	6,880 / 1,800,000	96 / 2.3	Kuwait	Arabic, English	Constitutional monarchy; Crown Prince Saad al-Abdullah al-Salim al-Sabah	1961 / 29	78/69 / 73/77	$16,900 / 0.84

COUNTRY	AREA (SQ MI) POPULATION	URBAN POP. (%) POP. ANNUAL RISE (%)	CAPITAL	MAJOR LANGUAGES	FORM OF GOVERNMENT[1] AND HEAD	DATE OF INDEP.[2] % OF POP. UNDER 15 YEARS	LITERACY RATE (%)[3] LIFE EXPECTANCY	PER-CAPITA GDP[4] HDI[5]
Kyrgyz Republic	76,640 / 4,600,000	35 / 1.6	Bishkek	Kirghiz, Russian	Presidential-parliamentary democracy; President Askar Akayev	1991 / 38	99/96 / 64/72	$1,790 / 0.66
Laos	89,110 / 5,000,000	19 / 2.9	Vientiane	Lao, French, English	Communist; President Nouhak Phoumsavan	1949 / 45	65/35 / 50/53	$850 / 0.40
Latvia	24,900 / 2,500,000	69 / -0.7	Riga	Lettish, Lithuanian, Russian, others	Presidential-parliamentary democracy; President Andris Skele	1991 / 21	100/99 / 61/73	$4,480 / 0.82
Lebanon	3,950 / 3,800,000	86 / 2.0	Beirut	Arabic, French, Armenian, English	Presidential-parliamentary with military influence President Ilyas Harawi	1943 / 33	88/73 / 73/78	$4,360 / 0.66
Lesotho	11,720 / 2,100,000	16 / 2.6	Maseru	Sesotho, English, Zulu, Xhosa	Parliamentary democracy; Prime Minister Ntsu Mokhehele	1966 / 41	44/68 / 54/57	$1,340 / 0.46
Liberia	37,190 / 2,100,000	44 / 3.1	Monrovia	English, Niger-Congo languages	Transitional; Council of State Chairperson Ruth Perry	1847 / 44	50/29 / 55/60	$770 / 0.31
Libya	679,360 / 5,400,000	85 / 3.7	Tripoli	Arabic, Italian, English	Military; Colonel Muammar al-Qaddafi	1951 / 45	77/42 / 62/66	$6,510 / 0.79
Liechtenstein	60 / 30,000	NA / 0.5	Vaduz	German, Alemannic dialect	Constitutional monarchy; Prince Hans Adam II	1719 / 19	100 / 68/75	$22,300 / NA
Lithuania	25,210 / 3,700,000	69 / -0.1	Vilnius	Lithuanian, Polish, Russian	Presidential-parliamentary democracy; Prime Minister Mindaugas Stankevicius	1991 / 22	99/98 / 63/75	$3,500 / 0.72
Luxembourg	990 / 400,000	86 / 0.4	Luxembourg	Luxembourgisch, German, French	Parliamentary democracy; Prime Minister Jean-Claude Juncker	1839 / 18	100 / 73/79	$22,830 / 0.90

M-Q

COUNTRY	AREA (SQ MI) POPULATION	URBAN POP. (%) POP. ANNUAL RISE (%)	CAPITAL	MAJOR LANGUAGES	FORM OF GOVERNMENT[1] AND HEAD	DATE OF INDEP.[2] % OF POP. UNDER 15 YEARS	LITERACY RATE (%)[3] LIFE EXPECTANCY	PER-CAPITA GDP[4] HDI[5]
Macedonia	9,930 / 2,100,000	58 / 0.8	Skopje	Macedonian, Albanian, others	Presidential-parliamentary democracy; President Kiro Gligorov	1991 / 24	NA / 70/74	$900 / NA
Madagascar	224,530 / 15,200,000	26 / 3.2	Antananarivo	French, Malagasy	Presidential-parliamentary democracy; President Albert Zafy	1960 / 46	88/73 / 55/58	$790 / 0.35
Malawi	36,320 / 9,500,000	17 / 3.0	Lilongwe	English, Chichewa, others	Presidential-parliamentary democracy; President Bakili Muluzi	1964 / 48	65/34 / 45/46	$750 / 0.32
Malaysia	126,850 / 20,600,000	51 / 2.4	Kuala Lumpur	Malay, English, others	Dominant party; Prime Minister Mahathir bin Mohamad	1957 / 36	86/70 / 70/75	$8,650 / 0.83
Maldives	120 / 300,000	26 / 3.6	Male	Divehi, English	President and legislature controlled by elite families; President Maumoon Abdul Gayoom	1965 / 47	91/92 / 63/66	$1,500 / 0.61
Mali	471,120 / 9,700,000	26 / 3.1	Bamako	French, Bambara, many others	Presidential-parliamentary democracy; President Alpha Oumar Konaré	1960 / 48	27/12 / 44/48	$600 / 0.22
Malta	120 / 400,000	89 / 0.6	Valletta	Maltese, English	Parliamentary democracy; Prime Minister Edward Fenech Adami	1964 / 22	86/82 / 75/79	$10,760 / 0.89
Marshall Islands	70 / 100,000	65 / 2.2	Majuro	English, Japanese, others	Parliamentary democracy; President Amata Kabua	1986 / 51	100/88 / 60/63	$1,500 / NA
Mauritania	395,840 / 2,300,000	39 / 2.5	Nouakchott	Hasaniya Arabic, Wolof, Pular, Soninke	Dominant party; President Maaouya Ould Sid'Ahmed Taya	1960 / 45	46/25 / 50/53	$1,110 / 0.35
Mauritius	710 / 1,100,000	44 / 1.3	Port Louis	English, Creole, French, others	Parliamentary democracy; Prime Minister Navin Ramgoolam	1968 / 29	85/75 / 65/73	$8,600 / 0.83
Mexico	736,950 / 94,800,000	71 / 2.2	Mexico City	Spanish, Indian languages	Dominant party; President Ernesto Zedillo Ponce de Léon	1810 / 36	90/85 / 70/76	$7,900 / 0.85

COUNTRY	AREA (SQ MI) / POPULATION	URBAN POP. (%) / POP. ANNUAL RISE (%)	CAPITAL	MAJOR LANGUAGES	FORM OF GOVERNMENT[1] AND HEAD	DATE OF INDEP.[2] / % OF POP. UNDER 15 YEARS	LITERACY RATE (%)[3] / LIFE EXPEC-TANCY	PER-CAPITA GDP[4] / HDI[5]
Micronesia	270 / 100,000	26 / 3.0	Palikir	English, Trukese, others	Parliamentary democracy; President Bailey Olter	1986 / 43	91/88 / 62/66	$1,500 / NA
Moldova	14,170 / 4,300,000	47 / 0.3	Chisinau (Kishinev)	Moldovan, Russian, Gagauz	Presidential-parliamentary democracy; President Mircea Snegur	1991 / 27	99/94 / 64/71	$2,670 / 0.66
Monaco	0.75 / 31,280	NA / 0.8	Monaco	French, English, Italian, Monegasque	Constitutional monarchy; Prince Rainier III	1419 / NA	NA / 74/82	$18,000 / NA
Mongolia	604,830 / 2,300,000	55 / 1.4	Ulaanbaatar (Ulan Bator)	Khalkha Mongol, Turkic, Russian, Chinese	Presidential-parliamentary democracy; Prime Minister Puntsagiyn Jasray	1921 / 40	NA / 62/65	$1,800 / 0.58
Morocco	172,320 / 27,600,000	47 / 2.2	Rabat	Arabic, Berber dialects, French	Constitutional monarchy; King Hassan II	1956 / 38	61/38 / 66/70	$3,060 / 0.53
Mozambique	302,740 / 16,500,000	33 / 2.7	Maputo	Portuguese, African languages	Presidential-legislative demoracy; President Joaquím Alberto Chissano	1975 / 46	45/21 / 45/48	$610 / 0.26
Myanmar (Burma)	253,880 / 46,000,000	25 / 1.9	Yangon (Rangoon)	Burmese, others	Military; General Than Shwe	1948 / 36	89/72 / 60/62	$930 / 0.45
Namibia	317,870 / 1,600,000	32 / 2.7	Windhoek	Afrikaans, German, English, others	Presidential-legislative democracy; President Sam Nujoma	1990 / 42	45/31 / 58/60	$3,600 / 0.57
Nauru	8 / 10,000	NA / 1.3	no official capital	Nauruan, English	Parliamentary democracy; President Lagumot Harris	1968 / NA	NA / 64/69	$10,000 / NA
Nepal	52,820 / 23,200,000	10 / 2.6	Kathmandu	Nepali, others	Parliamentary democracy; Prime Minister Sher Bahadur Deuba	1768 / 42	38/13 / 56/53	$1,060 / 0.33
Netherlands	13,100 / 15,500,000	61 / 0.4	Amsterdam	Dutch	Parliamentary democracy; Prime Minister Willem Kok	1579 / 18	99 / 74/80	$17,940 / 0.94
New Zealand	103,470 / 3,600,000	85 / 0.9	Wellington	English, Maori	Parliamentary democracy; Prime Minister James Bolger	1907 / 23	99 / 73/79	$16,640 / 0.93
Nicaragua	45,850 / 4,600,000	63 / 2.7	Managua	Spanish, English, Indian languages	Presidential-legislative democracy; President Violeta Chamorro	1821 / 44	57/57 / 62/68	$1,570 / 0.57
Niger	489,070 / 9,500,000	15 / 3.4	Niamey	French, Hausa, Djerma	Military; National Council President Bare Mainassara	1960 / 49	17/5 / 45/48	$550 / 0.21
Nigeria	351,650 / 103,900,000	16 / 3.1	Abuja	English, Hausa, Yoruba, Ibo, Fulani	Military; General Sani Abacha	1960 / 45	62/40 / 55/58	$1,250 / 0.40
Niue	100 / 1,900	NA / 3.7	Alofi	Polynesian (related to Tongan and Samoan), English	Parliamentary democracy; Premier Frank Lui	1974 / NA	NA / NA	$1,200 / NA
Norway	118,470 / 4,400,000	73 / 0.4	Oslo	Norwegian, Lapp, Finnish	Parliamentary democracy; Prime Minister Gro Harlem Brundtland	1905 / 19	99 / 75/81	$22,170 / 0.94
Oman	82,030 / 2,300,000	12 / 4.9	Muscat	Arabic, English, Baluchi, others	Monarchy; Prime Minister Sultan Qabus ibn Sa'id al Sa'id	1650 / 36	NA / 70/72	$10,020 / 0.72
Pakistan	297,640 / 133,500,000	28 / 2.9	Islamabad	Urdu, English, Punjabi, others	Presidential-parliamentary democracy; Prime Minister Benazir Bhutto	1947 / 41	47/21 / 61/61	$1,930 / 0.44
Palau	190 / 20,000	69 / 1.4	Koror	English, Angaur, Sonsorolese, Japanese, others	Presidential-legislative democracy; President Kuniwo Nakamura	1994 / 30	93/90 / NA	$5,000 / NA
Panama	29,340 / 2,700,000	55 / 1.8	Panama	Spanish, English	Presidential-legislative democracy; President Ernesto Pérez Balladares	1903 / 33	89/88 / 71/75	$4,670 / 0.86
Papua New Guinea	174,850 / 4,300,000	15 / 2.3	Port Moresby	English, pidgin English, Motu, many others	Parliamentary democracy; Prime Minister Julius Chan	1975 / 42	65/38 / 56/57	$2,200 / 0.50

COUNTRY	AREA (SQ MI) POPULATION	URBAN POP. (%) POP. ANNUAL RISE (%)	CAPITAL	MAJOR LANGUAGES	FORM OF GOVERNMENT[1] AND HEAD	DATE OF INDEP.[2] % OF POP. UNDER 15 YEARS	LITERACY RATE (%)[3] LIFE EXPEC-TANCY	PER-CAPITA GDP[4] HDI[5]
Paraguay	153,400 / 5,000,000	50 / 2.8	Asunción	Spanish, Guarani	Presidential-legislative democracy; President Juan Carlos Wasmosy	1811 / 42	92/88 / 66/71	$2,950 / 0.70
Peru	494,210 / 24,000,000	70 / 2.1	Lima	Spanish, Quechua, Aymara	Presidential dictatorship; President Alberto Kenyo Fujimori	1821 / 36	92/74 / 64/68	$3,110 / 0.70
Philippines	115,120 / 72,000,000	49 / 2.1	Manila	Pilipino, English	Presidential-legislative democracy; President Fidel Ramos	1946 / 38	94/93 / 63/66	$2,310 / 0.67
Poland	117,550 / 38,600,000	62 / 0.2	Warsaw	Polish	Presidential-parliamentary democracy; President Aleksander Kwasniewski	1918 / 23	99/98 / 68/76	$4,920 / 0.82
Portugal	35,500 / 9,900,000	48 / 0.1	Lisbon	Portuguese	Presidential-parliamentary democracy; Prime Minister Antonio Guterres	1910 / 18	89/82 / 71/78	$10,190 / 0.88
Qatar	4,250 / 700,000	91 / 1.6	Doha	Arabic, English	Monarchy; Amir and Prime Minister Khalifa ibn Hamad Al Thani	1971 / 30	77/72 / 70/75	$20,820 / 0.84

R-S

COUNTRY	AREA (SQ MI) POPULATION	URBAN POP. (%) POP. ANNUAL RISE (%)	CAPITAL	MAJOR LANGUAGES	FORM OF GOVERNMENT AND HEAD	DATE OF INDEP. % OF POP. UNDER 15 YEARS	LITERACY RATE (%) LIFE EXPEC-TANCY	PER-CAPITA GDP HDI
Romania	88,930 / 22,600,000	55 / -0.2	Bucharest	Romanian, Hungarian, German	Presidential-parliamentary democracy; President Nicolae Vacaroiu	1947 / 21	98/95 / 66/73	$2,790 / 0.74
Russia	6,592,800 / 147,700,000	73 / -0.5	Moscow	Russian, other languages	Presidential-parliamentary democracy; President Boris Yeltsin	1991 / 21	100/97 / 57/71	$4,820 / 0.80
Rwanda	9,530 / 6,900,000	5 / 2.7	Kigali	Kinyarwanda, French, Kiswahili	Dominant party; President Pasteur Bizimungu	1962 / 48	64/37 / 46/49	$950 / 0.33
Saint Kitts and Nevis	140 / 40,000	42 / 1.3	Basseterre	English	Parliamentary democracy; Prime Minister Denzil Douglas	1983 / 32	97/98 / 66/71	$5,300 / 0.86
Saint Lucia	240 / 100,000	48 / 2.0	Castries	English, French patois	Parliamentary democracy; Prime Minister John Compton	1979 / 37	65/69 / 69/75	$4,200 / 0.73
Saint Vincent and the Grenadines	150 / 100,000	25 / 1.8	Kingstown	English, French patois	Parliamentary democracy; Prime Minister James F. Mitchell	1979 / 37	96/96 / 71/74	$2,000 / 0.74
San Marino	20 / 30,000	91 / 0.3	San Marino	Italian	Parliamentary democracy; Secretary of State Gabriele Gatti	301 / 15	97/95 / 73/79	$15,800 / NA
São Tomé and Principe	370 / 100,000	46 / 2.6	São Tomé	Portuguese	Presidential-parliamentary democracy; President Miguel Trovoada	1975 / 47	85/62 / 62/65	$1,000 / 0.46
Saudi Arabia	830,000 / 19,400,000	79 / 3.2	Riyadh	Arabic	Monarchy; King and Prime Minister Fahd ibn Abd al-Aziz Al Sa'ud	1932 / 43	73/48 / 69/72	$9,510 / 0.77
Senegal	74,340 / 8,500,000	43 / 2.7	Dakar	French, Wolof, others	Dominant party; President Abdou Diouf	1960 / 45	37/18 / 48/50	$1,450 / 0.33
Serbia and Montenegro (Yugoslavia)	26,940 / 10,200,000	57 / 0.3	Belgrade	Serbo-Croatian, Albanian	Dominant party; Prime Minister Radoje Kontic[8]	1992 / 22	NA / 69/74	$1,000 / NA
Seychelles	100 / 100,000	50 / 1.5	Victoria	English, French, Creole	Presidential-legislative democracy; President France Albert René	1976 / 31	56/60 / 68/73	$6,000 / 0.79
Sierra Leone	27,650 / 4,600,000	35 / 2.7	Freetown	English, Krio, Mende, Temne	Military; President Ahmad Tejan Kabbah	1961 / 44	31/11 / 44/47	$1,000 / 0.22
Singapore	240 / 3,000,000	100 / 1.1	Singapore	Chinese, Malay, Tamil, English	Dominant party; Prime Minister Goh Chok Tong	1965 / 23	95/83 / 74/79	$19,940 / 0.88
Slovakia	18,790 / 5,400,000	57 / 0.3	Bratislava	Slovak, Hungarian	Parliamentary democracy; Prime Minister Vladimir Meciar	1993 / 23	NA / 68/77	$6,070 / 0.86

COUNTRY	AREA (SQ MI)	URBAN POP. (%)	CAPITAL	MAJOR LANGUAGES	FORM OF GOVERNMENT[1] AND HEAD	DATE OF INDEP.[2]	LITERACY RATE (%)[3]	PER-CAPITA GDP[4]
	POPULATION	POP. ANNUAL RISE (%)				% OF POP. UNDER 15 YEARS	LIFE EXPEC-TANCY	HDI[5]
Slovenia	7,820	50	Ljubljana	Slovenian, Serbo-Croatian, others	Presidential-parliamentary democracy; Prime Minister Janez Drnovsek	1991	NA	$8,110
	2,000,000	0.0				19	69/77	NA
Solomon Islands	10,810	13	Honiara	Melanesian pidgin, English, others	Parliamentary democracy; Prime Minister Solomon Mamaloni	1978	NA	$2,590
	400,000	3.4				47	68/73	0.56
Somalia	242,220	24	Mogadishu	Somali, Arabic, Italian, English	Rival warlords; no leader	1960	36/14	$500
	9,500,000	3.2				48	45/49	0.22
South Africa	471,440	57	Cape Town, Pretoria, and Bloemfontein	English, Afrikaans, Zulu, Xhosa, Sotho, others	Presidential-legislative democracy; President Nelson Mandela	1910	78/75	$4,420
	44,500,000	2.3				37	63/68	0.65
Spain	192,830	64	Madrid	Spanish, Catalan, Galician, Basque	Parliamentary democracy; Prime Minister José Maria Aznar	1492	98/94	$13,120
	39,300,000	0.1				17	73/81	0.93
Sri Lanka	24,950	22	Colombo	Sinhala, Tamil, English	Presidential-parliamentary democracy; President Chandrika Bandaranike Kumaratunga	1948	93/84	$3,190
	18,400,000	1.5				35	70/75	0.70
Sudan	917,370	27	Khartoum	Arabic, regional languages, English	Military; Lieutenant General Omar Hassan Ahmad al-'Bashir	1956	44/21	$870
	28,900,000	3.0				43	53/55	0.36
Suriname	60,230	49	Paramaribo	Dutch, English, Sranan Tongo	Presidential-parliamentary democracy; President Ronald R. Venetiaan	1975	95/95	$2,800
	400,000	1.6				35	68/73	0.74
Swaziland	6,640	30	Mbabane and Lobamba	English, siSwati	Monarchy; King Mswati III	1968	70/65	$3,490
	1,000,000	3.2				46	52/61	0.59
Sweden	158,930	83	Stockholm	Swedish, Lapp, Finnish	Parliamentary democracy; Prime Minister Goran Persson	1809	99	$18,580
	8,800,000	0.1				19	76/81	0.93
Switzerland	15,360	68	Bern	German, French, Italian, Romansch	Parliamentary democracy; President of Federal Council Jean-Pascal Delamuraz	1291	99	$22,080
	7,100,000	0.3				18	75/82	0.93
Syria	71,070	51	Damascus	Arabic, Kurdish, Armenian, others	Dominant party; President Hafez al-Assad	1946	78/51	$5,000
	15,600,000	3.7				49	65/67	0.69

T-Z

COUNTRY	AREA (SQ MI)	URBAN POP. (%)	CAPITAL	MAJOR LANGUAGES	FORM OF GOVERNMENT AND HEAD	DATE OF INDEP.	LITERACY RATE (%)	PER-CAPITA GDP
Taiwan	13,900	75	Taipei	Mandarin Chinese, Taiwanese, others	Presidential-legislative government moving toward democracy; President Lee Teng-hui	1947	93/79	$12,070
	21,400,000	1.0				24	72/77	NA
Tajikistan	54,290	28	Dushanbe	Tajik, Russian	Dominant party; President Emomili Rakhmanov	1991	99/97	$1,415
	5,900,000	2.1				43	65/71	0.62
Tanzania	342,100	21	Dar es Salaam	Swahili, English	Dominant party; Prime Minister Benjamin Mkapa	1964	71/48	$750
	29,100,000	3.0				47	47/50	0.36
Thailand	197,250	19	Bangkok	Thai, English, others	Parliamentary democracy; Prime Minister Chuan Leekpai	1238	96/91	$5,970
	60,700,000	1.4				30	68/72	0.83
Togo	21,000	30	Lomé	French, Ewe, Mina, Dagomba, Kabye	Military; President General Gnassingbé Eyadéma	1960	56/31	$800
	4,600,000	3.6				49	55/59	0.39
Tonga	301	NA	Nuku'alofa	Tongan, English	Constitutional monarchy; King Taufa'ahau Tupou IV	1970	100	$2,050
	104,780	0.8				NA	65/70	NA
Trinidad and Tobago	1,980	65	Port-of-Spain	English, Hindi, French, Spanish	Parliamentary democracy; Prime Minister Patrick Manning	1962	98/96	$11,280
	1,300,000	1.2				31	68/73	0.87
Tunisia	59,980	60	Tunis	Arabic, French	Dominant party; President Zine el-Abidine Ben Ali	1956	69/45	$4,250
	9,200,000	1.7				37	67/69	0.73
Turkey	297,150	63	Ankara	Turkish, Kurdish, Arabic	Presidential-parliamentary democracy; Prime Minister Necmettin Erbakan	1923	90/68	$4,910
	63,900,000	1.6				33	65/70	0.71

COUNTRY	AREA (SQ MI)	URBAN POP. (%)	CAPITAL	MAJOR LANGUAGES	FORM OF GOVERNMENT[1] AND HEAD	DATE OF INDEP.[2]	LITERACY RATE (%)[3]	PER-CAPITA GDP[4]
	POPULATION	POP. ANNUAL RISE (%)				% OF POP. UNDER 15 YEARS	LIFE EXPEC- TANCY	HDI[5]
Turkmenistan	188,500	45	Ashgabat	Turkmen, Russian, Uzbek, others	Dominant party; President Saparmurad Niyazov	1991	99/97	$3,280
	4,600,000	2.4				41	62/69	0.70
Tuvalu	9.4	NA	Funafuti	Tuvaluan, English	Parliamentary democracy; Prime Minister Kamuta Latasi	1978	NA	$800
	9,830	1.7				NA	62/64	NA
Uganda	77,050	11	Kampala	English, Luganda, Swahili, others	Dominant party; President Yoweri Kaguta Museveni	1962	68/45	$850
	22,000,000	3.3				47	44/46	0.33
Ukraine	233,100	68	Kiev	Ukrainian, Russian, Romanian, Polish	Presidential-parliamentary democracy; President Leonid Kuchma	1991	100/97	$3,650
	51,100,000	-0.5				20	63/73	0.72
United Arab Emirates	32,280	82	Abu Dhabi	Arabic, Persian, English, others	Federation of traditional monarchies; President Zayid ibn Sultan al-Nahayan	1971	72/69	$22,480
	1,900,000	1.9				32	70/74	0.86
United Kingdom (Great Britain)	93,280	90	London	English, Welsh, Scottish Gaelic	Parliamentary democracy; Prime Minister John Major	1801	99	$17,980
	58,800,000	0.2				19	74/79	0.92
United States	3,539,230	75	Washington, D.C.	English, Spanish, others	Presidential-legislative democracy; President Bill Clinton	1776	97/97	$25,850
	265,200,000	0.6				22	72/79	0.94
Uruguay	67,490	90	Montevideo	Spanish, Brazilero	Presidential-legislative democracy; President Julio Maria Sanguinetti	1828	97/96	$7,200
	3,200,000	0.8				26	69/76	0.88
Uzbekistan	172,740	39	Tashkent	Uzbek, Russian, Tajik, others	Dominant party; President Islam Karimov	1991	98/96	$2,400
	23,200,000	2.3				41	66/72	0.68
Vanuatu	4,710	18	Port-Vila	English, French, Bislama	Parliamentary democracy; Prime Minister Maxime Carlot Korman	1980	57/48	$1,200
	200,000	2.9				44	NA	0.56
Vatican City	109 acres	NA	Vatican City	Italian, Latin, others	No political parties; papal state; Pope John Paul II	1929	100	NA
	821	1.2				—	NA	NA
Venezuela	340,560	84	Caracas	Spanish, Indian languages	Presidential-legislative democracy; President Rafael Caldera Rodriguez	1811	91/89	$8,670
	22,300,000	2.1				38	69/75	0.86
Vietnam	125,670	19	Hanoi	Vietnamese, French, Chinese, others	Communist; Prime Minister Vo Van Kiet	1976	93/83	$1,140
	76,600,000	2.3				40	63/67	0.52
Western Samoa	1,090	21	Apia	Samoan, English	Parliamentary democracy; Chief of State Malietoa Tanumafili II	1962	97/97	$2,000
	200,000	2.3				41	NA	0.70
Yemen	203,850	23	Sanaa	Arabic	Two-party coalition; President Lieutenant General Ali Abdullah Salih	1990	53/26	$1,955
	14,700,000	3.2				52	51/53	0.37
Zaire	875,520	29	Kinshasa	French, Lingala, Swahili, others	Presidential-military; President Mobutu Sese Seko	1960	84/61	$440
	46,500,000	3.2				48	46/50	0.37
Zambia	287,020	42	Lusaka	English, many African languages	Presidential-parliamentary democracy; President Frederick Chiluba	1964	81/65	$860
	9,200,000	3.0				47	48/50	0.41
Zimbabwe	149,290	31	Harare	English, Shona, Sindebele	Dominant party; President Robert Mugabe	1980	84/72	$1,580
	11,500,000	2.5				45	61/62	0.53

NOTES

NA: Means figure(s) not available. [1]**Form of government and head:** Some countries have two heads: a head of state and a head of government. These tables list only the latter. (For instance, Queen Elizabeth is Britain's head of state, but John Major runs the government.) [2]**Date of independence:** The most recent year in which a country won control of its internal and external affairs, or when smaller areas joined to form a larger nation. [3]**Literacy rate:** Experts doubt some estimates. [4]**Per-capita gross domestic product:** Given in U.S. dollars. [5]**Human Development Index:** A number from zero to one, based on how a country's people fare in terms of life expectancy, adult literacy, and purchasing power (a person's ability to buy food, clothing, and other necessities). The higher the number, the better the rating. [6]After its September 1996 elections, Bosnia switched to a three-member collective presidency (one Croat, one Muslim, one Serb), with one president—winner of the most votes—serving as chairman. [7]Figures do not include the Gaza Strip or the West Bank, which are in transition to Palestinian control. [8]Serbia has its own president (Slobodan Milosevic), as does Montenegro (Momir Bulatovic). Together, under the name Yugoslavia, they have a government headed by Prime Minister Radoje Kontic. The state of Yugoslavia has not been formally recognized as a country.

SOURCES

For area, population, urban population, population annual rise, percent of population under 15 years, and life expectancy: *1996 World Population Data Sheet* (Population Reference Bureau, Inc.) • For capital, major languages, date of independence, literacy rate, and per-capita GDP: *The World Factbook 1995* (Central Intelligence Agency) • For form of government: *Freedom in the World: 1995-1996* (Freedom House) and information from the U.S. Department of State. • For head of government: *The Statesman's Yearbook, 1996-97* (St. Martin's Press), *The World Factbook 1995*, and information from the U.S. Department of State. • For HDI: *Human Development Report 1996* (United Nations Development Program)
The form of government and head information is up-to-date as of September 20, 1996.

4. The U.S. in Focus

You live in the U.S., but how much do you know about it? Who are the movers and shakers who head the federal government's three branches? Which of the 50 states has a name that means *sky-tinted waters*? What territory did the U.S. buy from Denmark for $25 million?

If you don't know the answers off the top of your head, no problem. They are all in this table—Part 1 of the U.S. in Focus section. These three pages provide a wealth of information about the 50 states, the District of Columbia, and U.S. territories and commonwealths. Happy exploring!

Area: 3,536,338 square miles; ranks fourth[1] in the world.
Population: 260,341,000; ranks third[2] in the world.
Capital: Washington, D.C.
Form of Government: Presidential-legislative democracy. The U.S. Constitution divides **federal** (national) powers among three independent branches of government: the legislative, the executive, and the judicial. Powers not given to the federal government by the Constitution are held by the states.
Chief Justice of the U.S.: William H. Rehnquist.

State Name / Nickname	Origin of Name	Entered Union	Land Area (sq mi) / Population	Capital
ALABAMA The Heart of Dixie	Named for Alibamu Indian tribes	1819	50,750 / 4,219,000	**Montgomery**
ALASKA The Last Frontier (unofficial)	Russian version of an Aleut word	1959	570,374 / 606,000	
ARIZONA The Grand Canyon State	Indian word *arizonac*, means *small spring*	1912	113,642 / 4,075,000	**Phoenix**
ARKANSAS The Land of Opportunity	From an Indian word meaning *land of downstream people*	1836	52,075 / 2,453,000	**Little Rock**
CALIFORNIA The Golden State	After a treasure island in a popular Spanish tale	1850	155,973 / 31,431,000	**Sacramento**
COLORADO The Centennial State	Spanish for *colored red*	1876	103,729 / 3,656,000	**Denver**
CONNECTICUT The Constitution State	Algonquian Indian word; means *on the long tidal river*	1788	4,845 / 3,275,000	**Hartford**
DELAWARE The First State	Honors Lord De La Warre, first governor, Virginia Colony	1787	1,955 / 706,000	**Dover**
FLORIDA The Sunshine State	Spanish word for *flowery*	1845	53,997 / 13,953,000	**Tallahassee**
GEORGIA The Empire State of the South	Honors King George II of Great Britain	1788	57,919 / 7,055,000	**Atlanta**
HAWAII The Aloha State	Native word for *homeland*	1959	6,423 / 1,179,000	**Honolulu**
IDAHO The Gem State	Word invented to mean *gem of the mountains*	1890	82,751 / 1,133,000	**Boise**
ILLINOIS The Prairie State	For Iliniwek Indians; name means *superior men*	1818	55,593 / 11,752,000	**Springfield**
INDIANA The Hoosier State	Word *indian* plus suffix *a*	1816	35,870 / 5,752,000	**Indianapolis**
IOWA The Hawkeye State	Indian word for *beautiful land*	1846	55,875 / 2,829,000	**Des Moines**

State Name / Nickname	Origin of Name	Entered Union	Land Area (sq mi) / Population	Capital
KANSAS The Sunflower State	For Kansa Indians; name means *people of the south wind*	1861	81,823 2,554,000	**Topeka**
KENTUCKY The Bluegrass State	Cherokee word for *meadowland*	1792	39,732 3,827,000	**Frankfort**
LOUISIANA The Pelican State	Honors Louis XIV, king of France	1812	43,566 4,315,000	**Baton Rouge**
MAINE The Pine Tree State	Honors ancient French province of Maine	1820	30,865 1,240,000	**Augusta**
MARYLAND The Old Line State; The Free State	Honors Queen Henrietta Maria of England	1788	9,775 5,006,000	**Annapolis**
MASSACHUSETTS The Bay State	For Massachuset Indians; name means *near the great hill*	1788	7,838 6,041,000	**Boston**
MICHIGAN The Wolverine State	Chippewa word *Michigama;* means *great water*	1837	56,809 9,496,000	**Lansing**
MINNESOTA The North Star State	Sioux Indian word for *sky-tinted waters*	1858	79,617 4,567,000	**St. Paul**
MISSISSIPPI The Magnolia State	Indian word meaning *father of waters*	1817	46,914 2,669,000	**Jackson**
MISSOURI The Show Me State	Indian word meaning *town of the large canoes*	1821	68,898 5,278,000	**Jefferson City**
MONTANA The Treasure State	Spanish word for *mountainous*	1889	145,556 856,000	**Helena**
NEBRASKA The Cornhusker State	Oto Indian word *nebrathka;* means *flat water*	1867	76,878 1,623,000	**Lincoln**
NEVADA The Silver State	Spanish word for *snow-clad*	1864	109,806 1,457,000	**Carson City**
NEW HAMPSHIRE The Granite State	Named for Hampshire, a county in England	1788	8,969 1,137,000	**Concord**
NEW JERSEY The Garden State	Named for Jersey, an island in England	1787	7,419 7,904,000	**Trenton**
NEW MEXICO The Land of Enchantment	For Aztec Indian war god Mexitil	1912	121,364 1,654,000	**Santa Fe**
NEW YORK The Empire State	Honors England's Duke of York	1788	47,224 18,169,000	**Albany**
NORTH CAROLINA The Tar Heel State	Honors King Charles I of Great Britain	1789	48,718 7,070,000	**Raleigh**
NORTH DAKOTA The Peace Garden State	Named for Dakota Sioux Indians of the region	1889	68,994 638,000	**Bismarck**
OHIO The Buckeye State	Iroquois Indian word; means *something great*	1803	40,953 11,102,000	**Columbus**
OKLAHOMA The Sooner State	Choctaw Indian words *okla,* meaning *people,* and *homma,* meaning *red*	1907	68,679 3,258,000	**Oklahoma City**
OREGON The Beaver State	French word *ouragan;* means *hurricane*	1859	96,002 3,086,000	**Salem**
PENNSYLVANIA The Keystone State	Honors Sir William Penn (father of the founder of the colony), plus the Latin word for *woods*	1787	44,820 12,052,000	**Harrisburg**
RHODE ISLAND Little Rhody; The Ocean State	After the Greek isle of Rhodes (for its red clay)	1790	1,045 997,000	**Providence**

State Name / Nickname	Origin of Name	Entered Union	Land Area (sq mi) / Population	Capital
SOUTH CAROLINA The Palmetto State	Honors King Charles I of Great Britain	1788	30,111 3,664,000	Columbia
SOUTH DAKOTA The Coyote State	Named for Dakota Sioux Indians of the region	1889	75,896 721,000	Pierre
TENNESSEE The Volunteer State	From *Tanasie*, name of a Cherokee village	1796	41,219 5,175,000	Nashville
TEXAS The Lone Star State	From Caddo Indian word; means *friends*	1845	261,914 18,378,000	Austin
UTAH The Beehive State	Named for Ute Indians of the region	1896	82,168 1,908,000	Salt Lake City
VERMONT The Green Mountain State	French words *vert mont*, mean *green mountain*	1791	9,249 580,000	Montpelier
VIRGINIA The Old Dominion	Honors "the Virgin Queen," Great Britain's Elizabeth I	1788	39,598 6,552,000	Richmond
WASHINGTON The Evergreen State	Named after George Washington	1889	66,581 5,343,000	Olympia
WEST VIRGINIA The Mountain State	Honors "the Virgin Queen," Great Britain's Elizabeth I	1863	24,087 1,822,000	Charleston
WISCONSIN The Badger State	Chippewa word *ouisconsin*, means *grassy place*	1848	54,314 5,082,000	Madison
WYOMING The Equality State; The Cowboy State	From Delaware Indian word meaning *upon the great plain*	1890	97,105 476,000	Cheyenne

Capital District, Territories, and Commonwealths

Name	Origin of Name	Status / Date Acquired	Area (sq mi) / Population	Capital
DISTRICT OF COLUMBIA (D.C.)	Honors Christopher Columbus	Capital district[5] 1800[6]	61 570,000	Washington
AMERICAN SAMOA	Ancient Pacific deity	U.S. territory 1900[7]	77 46,700	Pago Pago
GUAM	From Guajan; in local dialect, means *We have*	U.S. territory 1898[8]	210 133,000	Agana
NORTHERN MARIANA ISLANDS	Honors Mariana of Austria, Regent of Spain	Self-governing commonwealth 1947[9]	179 43,000	Saipan
PUERTO RICO	Spanish for *rich port*	Self-governing commonwealth 1898[10]	3,427 3,522,000	San Juan
U.S. VIRGIN ISLANDS	Virgins of St. Ursula, early religious order; patron saint of Spanish sailors	U.S. territory 1917[12]	134 102,000	Charlotte Amalie

FOOTNOTES

[1]After Russia, China, and Canada. [2]After China and India. [3]A Jan. 30 election in Oregon will fill one Senate seat; a special election in California will fill one House seat. [4]I is for Independent (no political party). [5]Seat of the U.S. government. [6]Date when the federal government moved from Philadelphia to Washington. [7]Date gained by treaty with the U.K. and Germany. [8]Date ceded to the U.S. by Spain after the Spanish-American War; became a U.S. territory in 1950. [9]Date administration by the U.S. began (in a trusteeship for the United Nations); became a self-governing commonwealth in 1978. [10]Date became a U.S. territory; became a self-governing commonwealth in 1952. [11]NPP stands for New Progressive Party. [12]Purchased from Denmark for $25 million.

SOURCES

For nickname, date entered union/date acquired, and capital: *The Book of the States*, 1994-95 edition (Lexington, KY: The Council of State Governments, 1994) • **For origin of name:** *The World Book Encyclopedia*, 1992 edition • **For land area (1990) and population (1994):** *Statistical Abstract of the United States, 1995* (Washington, D.C.: U.S. Department of Commerce, Bureau of the Census, 1995) • **For governor/head of government:** National Governors' Association, the U.S. Department of the Interior, and the Puerto Rico Federal Affairs Administration • **For U.S. senators and representatives:** *The Congressional Quarterly*

The quality of life where you live is affected by many things. Is employment rising or falling? How much do people earn? How many of the tax dollars that they pay are put to work in your state? These are just a few of the factors to consider. Another factor: How do conditions in your state compare with those in the rest of the country?

This table—Part 2 of the U.S. in Focus section—can help you answer those questions and many others. (What others? Use your imagination, and you are sure to think of some!)

As you explore the data on these two pages, remember: Although **statistics** (a collection of measurable data) can be useful, they cannot tell the whole story. For instance, this table can tell you *which* state had the highest job-growth rate in the U.S. for 1989-1994, but it cannot tell you *why*.

Put on your thinking cap and poke around. How much can you find out about the 50 states, D.C., and the U.S. as a whole? Then ask yourself: What does this table *not* tell me? Where can I find the answers?

	Population change, 1990-94	Population in metropolitan areas, 1992[1]	Population under 18 years of age, 1994[2]	Population age 65 and over, 1994	Personal income per capita, 1994[3]	Population living in poverty, 1994[4]	Job growth, 1989-94[5]	Federal taxes paid per capita, 1994	U.S. federal spending per capita, 1994[6]	Public-school spending per student, 1994-95	Students who dropped out of high school, 1990[7]	Violent crimes per 100,000 people, 1994[8]
THE U.S.	4.7%	79.7%	26.1%	12.7%	$21,809	14.5%	5.7%	$4,728	$4,935	$5,442	11.2%	716.0
ALABAMA	4.4%	67.4%	25.6%	13.1%	$18,010	16.4%	9.4%	$3,691	$5,273	$4,194	12.6%	683.7
ALASKA	10.2%	41.8%	31.7%	4.6%	$23,788	10.2%	14.6%	$5,585	$7,703	$8,120	9.6%	766.3
ARIZONA	11.2%	84.7%	28.0%	13.4%	$19,001	15.9%	15.9%	$3,832	$4,693	$3,982	14.3%	703.1
ARKANSAS	4.3%	44.7%	26.1%	14.8%	$16,898	15.3%	15.9%	$3,525	$4,627	$3,795	10.9%	595.1
CALIFORNIA	5.6%	96.7%	27.6%	10.6%	$22,493	17.9%	-0.8%	$4,905	$4,960	$4,606	14.3%	1,013.0
COLORADO	11.0%	81.8%	26.5%	10.1%	$22,333	9.0%	18.0%	$4,931	$5,205	$5,101	9.6%	509.6
CONNECTICUT	-0.4%	95.7%	24.1%	14.2%	$29,402	10.8%	-7.4%	$7,300	$5,055	$8,147	9.2%	455.5
DELAWARE	6.0%	82.7%	24.8%	12.7%	$22,828	8.3%	3.0%	$5,665	$4,181	$6,591	11.2%	561.0
D.C.	-6.1%	100.0%	20.9%	13.5%	$31,136	21.2%	-3.4%	$6,896	$37,962	$7,520	19.1%	2,662.6
FLORIDA	7.8%	93.0%	23.4%	18.4%	$21,677	14.9%	10.2%	$4,771	$5,120	$5,185	14.2%	1,146.8
GEORGIA	8.9%	67.7%	26.8%	10.1%	$20,251	14.0%	11.0%	$4,203	$4,557	$4,595	14.1%	667.7
HAWAII	6.3%	74.7%	25.8%	12.1%	$24,057	8.7%	6.1%	$5,104	$6,457	$5,740	7.0%	262.2
IDAHO	12.5%	30.0%	29.9%	11.6%	$18,231	12.0%	26.6%	$3,782	$4,386	$3,976	9.6%	285.8
ILLINOIS	2.8%	84.0%	26.2%	12.6%	$23,784	12.4%	4.8%	$5,390	$4,238	$4,752	10.4%	960.9
INDIANA	3.8%	71.6%	25.6%	12.8%	$20,378	13.7%	9.4%	$4,240	$3,834	$5,158	11.4%	525.1
IOWA	1.9%	43.8%	25.8%	15.4%	$20,265	10.7%	9.9%	$4,008	$4,570	$5,139	6.5%	315.1
KANSAS	3.1%	54.6%	27.0%	13.9%	$20,896	14.9%	9.6%	$4,495	$4,889	$5,318	8.4%	478.7
KENTUCKY	3.8%	48.5%	25.3%	12.8%	$17,807	18.5%	11.6%	$3,603	$4,563	$5,007	13.0%	605.3
LOUISIANA	2.2%	75.0%	28.6%	11.4%	$17,651	25.7%	12.3%	$3,597	$5,002	$4,525	11.9%	981.9
MAINE	1.0%	35.7%	24.7%	13.9%	$19,663	9.4%	-2.0%	$3,864	$5,404	$6,048	8.4%	129.9
MARYLAND	4.7%	92.8%	25.2%	11.2%	$24,933	10.7%	-0.5%	$5,478	$7,311	$6,212	11.0%	948.0
MASSACHUSETTS	0.4%	96.2%	23.6%	14.1%	$25,616	9.7%	-6.5%	$5,754	$5,843	$6,383	9.5%	707.6

Data compiled by Kathy Wilmore

	Popula-tion change, 1990-94	Popula-tion in metro-politan areas, 1992[1]	Popula-tion under 18 years of age, 1994[2]	Popula-tion age 65 and over, 1994	Personal income per capita, 1994[3]	Popula-tion living in poverty 1994[4]	Job growth, 1989-94[5]	Federal taxes paid per capita, 1994	U.S. federal spending per capi-ta, 1994[6]	Public-school spending per student, 1994-95	Students who dropped out of high school, 1990[7]	Violent crimes per 100,000 people, 1994[8]
MICHIGAN	2.2%	82.7%	26.6%	12.4%	$22,333	14.1%	5.6%	$4,765	$4,093	$6,240	9.9%	766.1
MINNESOTA	4.4%	69.3%	27.2%	12.5%	$22,453	11.7%	10.8%	$4,930	$4,113	$5,413	6.1%	359.0
MISSISSIPPI	3.6%	34.6%	28.3%	12.5%	$15,838	19.9%	14.6%	$2,980	$5,262	$3,469	11.7%	493.7
MISSOURI	3.1%	68.3%	26.1%	14.1%	$20,717	15.6%	6.8%	$4,314	$6,008	$4,502	11.2%	743.5
MONTANA	7.1%	24.0%	27.8%	13.3%	$17,865	11.5%	17.0%	$3,823	$5,411	$5,091	7.1%	177.1
NEBRASKA	2.8%	50.6%	27.2%	14.1%	$20,488	8.8%	12.4%	$4,302	$4,572	$5,018	6.6%	389.5
NEVADA	21.2%	84.8%	25.8%	11.3%	$24,023	11.1%	26.8%	$5,262	$4,233	$4,677	14.9%	1,001.9
NEW HAMPSHIRE	2.5%	59.4%	25.7%	11.9%	$23,434	7.7%	-1.3%	$5,169	$4,084	$5,845	9.9%	116.8
NEW JERSEY	2.2%	100.0%	24.4%	13.6%	$28,038	9.2%	-3.8%	$6,482	$4,715	$9,206	9.3%	614.2
NEW MEXICO	9.1%	56.0%	30.1%	11.0%	$17,106	21.1%	17.1%	$3,477	$6,831	$4,870	10.8%	889.2
NEW YORK	1.0%	91.7%	24.8%	13.2%	$25,999	17.0%	-5.4%	$5,817	$4,960	$8,217	10.1%	965.6
NORTH CAROLINA	6.6%	66.3%	24.8%	12.5%	$19,669	14.2%	9.3%	$4,001	$4,085	$4,739	13.2%	655.0
NORTH DAKOTA	-0.1%	41.6%	27.0%	14.7%	$18,546	10.4%	13.2%	$3,762	$6,103	$4,459	4.3%	81.8
OHIO	2.4%	81.3%	25.7%	13.4%	$20,928	14.1%	5.4%	$4,543	$4,314	$5,452	8.8%	485.8
OKLAHOMA	3.6%	60.1%	27.0%	13.6%	$17,744	16.7%	9.9%	$3,677	$4,817	$4,042	9.9%	651.5
OREGON	8.6%	70.0%	25.4%	13.7%	$20,419	11.8%	13.1%	$4,345	$4,232	$5,710	11.0%	520.6
PENNSYLVANIA	1.4%	84.8%	24.0%	15.9%	$22,324	12.5%	1.0%	$4,859	$5,049	$6,909	9.4%	426.7
RHODE ISLAND	-0.7%	93.6%	24.1%	15.6%	$22,251	10.3%	-6.0%	$4,977	$5,478	$6,729	12.9%	375.5
SOUTH CAROLINA	5.1%	69.8%	26.0%	11.9%	$17,695	13.8%	7.2%	$3,587	$4,668	$4,401	11.9%	1,030.5
SOUTH DAKOTA	3.6%	32.6%	28.8%	14.7%	$19,577	14.5%	20.6%	$3,926	$5,279	$4,693	7.1%	227.6
TENNESSEE	6.1%	67.7%	25.1%	12.7%	$19,482	14.6%	11.7%	$4,144	$4,839	$4,208	13.6%	747.9
TEXAS	8.2%	83.9%	28.8%	10.2%	$19,857	19.1%	13.2%	$4,287	$4,326	$4,894	12.5%	706.5
UTAH	10.7%	77.5%	35.2%	8.8%	$17,043	8.0%	24.6%	$3,408	$3,991	$3,431	7.9%	304.5
VERMONT	3.1%	27.0%	25.2%	12.1%	$20,224	7.6%	0.8%	$4,246	$4,155	$6,879	8.7%	96.9
VIRGINIA	5.9%	77.5%	24.5%	11.1%	$22,594	10.7%	5.0%	$4,830	$7,013	$5,303	10.4%	357.7
WASHINGTON	9.8%	83.0%	26.4%	11.6%	$22,610	11.7%	12.8%	$5,123	$4,999	$5,563	10.2%	511.3
WEST VIRGINIA	1.6%	41.8%	23.5%	15.4%	$17,208	18.6%	9.8%	$3,309	$5,216	$5,565	10.6%	215.8
WISCONSIN	3.9%	68.1%	26.5%	13.4%	$21,019	9.0%	11.0%	$4,505	$3,864	$6,358	6.9%	270.5
WYOMING	4.9%	29.7%	28.8%	11.1%	$20,436	9.3%	12.5%	$4,524	$4,909	$5,582	6.3%	272.5

FOOTNOTES

[1]Percentage of a state's people living in a metropolitan area. (A *metropolitan area* is a heavily populated city and surrounding communities that have close economic and social ties with the city.) [2]Figures are estimates. [3]Income received from all sources during the year, divided by the population. (*Per capita* means *per person.*) [4]The percentage of persons whose income falls below the poverty line of each state. (The poverty line varies, depending on the size of families and other factors. In 1994, the national poverty line for a family of four was $15,141.) [5]Farm payroll employment not included. [6]The amount that the U.S. government spent in a state, divided by the number of people in that state. [7]Ages 16-19. [8]Violent crimes are offenses of murder, forcible rape, robbery, and aggravated assault.

SOURCES

For poverty rate: U.S. Department of Commerce, Bureau of the Census ● **For job growth:** Bureau of Labor Statistics, U.S. Department of Labor ● **For federal taxes paid per capita and U.S. federal spending per capita:** Tax Foundation ● **For public school spending per student:** National Education Association ● **For dropout rate:** U.S. Department of Education ● **For violent crimes per 100,000 people:** Federal Bureau of Investigation (FBI) ● **For all other categories:** *Statistical Abstract of the United States: 1995* (Washington, D.C.: U.S. Bureau of the Census, 1994)

INDEX